Contents

GW00602767

Diamond
Publications

© Copyright

Published by Diamond Publications, PO Box 59, Bideford, Devon EX39 4YN

Editor: Graham Sleeman	(01566) 785782
Distribution: Harry Lentern	(01271) 858528
Advertising: Jane Diamond	(01271) 860183
Design & Typeset by Type High:	(01566) 785782
Printed by Brightsea Press	(01392) 360616
Cover Picture: Chris Robbins Photography	(01566) 784259

Special thanks to the team at the Environment Agency, Mike Weaver, Gav' for inputting data, annually understanding partners and children and everyone who contributed to this, the fifth of many. Best one yet!

While every effort has been made to ensure that the information in this publication is accurate at the time of going to press, the publishers cannot accept responsibility for any errors or omissions which may have occurred. Remember fisheries change hands and rules change. Always phone if in doubt.

ISBN 0 9527547 2 X

Introduction

Welcome...

To the fifth, even bigger and more comprehensive edition.

This year sees us continuing our successful association with the Environment Agency.

Once again we have contacted EVERY fishery and association, offering day ticket fishing, known to us or the Environment Agency, throughout the area. Everyone who has responded is detailed in our listings section which has doubled in size.

In fact every section of the guide has increased in size re-affirming our position as THE DEFINITIVE guide to angling throughout the South West of England.

May we take this annual opportunity to ask those who have not responded or whom we don't know of, to contact us for insertion in next year's issue.

We have various editorials from local sources extolling the virtues of angling in the South West as well as the Environment Agency's contribution, which details all of the latest local fishery byelaws, seasons etc. This years guide includes, amongst others, contributions from The Westcountry Rivers Trust, The Angling Trade Association and The Salmon and Trout Association. All organisations which exist to preserve and promote our sport, ever more important as more questions are asked over the morals of fishing.

Our thanks again to all the advertisers and contributors who make this publication what it is. We know the advertising is successful and hope the new advertisers will benefit as much as those who have been with us from issue one. Thanks also to our editorial contributors, we couldn't find space for all of you but your efforts are much appreciated.

As ever our pages are graced with many photographs kindly supplied from fisheries throughout the region. We would like to reiterate that the vast majority of pictures are supplied by anglers and fishery owners, not photographers.

From some of the best sea fishing to a huge variety of coarse fishing and game fishing, on stillwaters and rivers, to equal anywhere in the country. The South West has a lot to offer anglers from all branches of the sport.

We are sure you will find The Get Hooked Guide to Angling in the South West of England useful, informative and entertaining, whether you are local or visiting the area.

Enjoy your fishing

Graham Sleeman
Editor.

Editor catches a fish! See story on page 86

ENVIRONMENT AGENCY

Bringing together a number of environmental bodies, the Environment Agency took up its operational role as environmental watchdog and enforcer on 1 April 1996.

The Agency's primary aim is to protect and improve the environment and make a contribution towards the delivery of sustainable development through the integrated management of air, land and water.

It has specific responsibilities for water resources, pollution prevention and control, flood defence, fisheries, conservation and recreation.

The vision of the Agency is "a better environment in England and Wales for present and future generations."

A key element in this vision is looking after the important fisheries of the South West.

Fish are one of the best indicators of the state of rivers and lakes. Healthy and abundant freshwater fish stocks and populations will demonstrate the Agency's success in contributing towards its overarching duty to contribute towards sustainable development.

To help make progress, Local Environment Agency Plans or LEAPs and

salmon action plans or SAPs are being drawn up with the help of public consultation for the whole region.

These include lists of actions for the Agency and other interested parties to protect and enhance the environment. Copies of these plans are available free of charge from Agency offices.

The work of the Agency helps fisheries in many ways. Pollution prevention, dealing with low river flows and habitat improvements are three good examples.

In addition, the Agency's fisheries staff carry out a number of vital tasks.

These include
• Controlling the pressure on fisheries through issuing licences and making byelaws
• Preventing damage to fish and fish stocks by effective enforcement of fishery laws
• Ensuring the health and abundance of fish stocks through regular fisheries surveys
• Rescuing fish when pollution incidents occur and minimising damage to fish stocks
• Stocking fish to restore and improve fisheries
• Carrying out habitat improvement
• Constructing fish passes
• Monitoring of fish stocks i.e. catch returns, juvenile surveys and fish counters
• Carrying out fisheries research to allow future improvements and developments

Fisheries operations are organised by staff based in the Agency's four South West areas.

They can be contacted as follows:

Cornwall:
Fisheries, Ecology and
Recreation Manager
Environment Agency
Sir John Moore House
Victoria Square
BODMIN PL31 1EB
Tel: 01208 78301
Fax: 01208 78321

Devon:

Fisheries, Ecology and
Recreation Manager
Environment Agency
Exminster House
Miller Way
EXMINSTER EX6 8AS
Tel: 01392 444000
Fax: 01392 316016

North Wessex:

Fisheries, Ecology and
Recreation Manager
Environment Agency
Rivers House
East Quay
BRIDGWATER Som. TA6 4YS
Tel: 01278 457333
Fax: 01278 452985

South Wessex:

Fisheries, Ecology and
Recreation Manager
Environment Agency
Rivers House
Sunrise Business Park
Higher Shaftesbury Road
BLANDFORD DT11 8ST
Tel: 01258 456080
Fax: 01258 455998

Strategic policy and planning issues are co-ordinated by fisheries staff at the Regional Office (Manley House, Exeter).

The Region is advised by the South West Regional Fisheries Advisory Committee. The Committee usually sits four times a year and its meetings are open to the public and the media. Local fisheries forums also meet in each of the four areas.

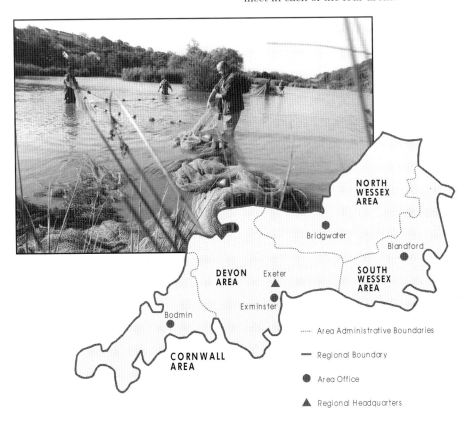

National Rod Licences

Before fishing for salmon, trout or freshwater fish (including eels) in any* water in England and Wales, it is necessary to have both a current Agency rod fishing licence and permission to fish from the owner of the fishery.

Except in waters where a general licence is in force - please check with the owner of the fishery in advance.

The area where a rod licence is required for fishing for salmon, trout and freshwater fish includes estuaries and the sea out to six miles from the shore.

In most cases a licence is not required to fish for freshwater eels in tidal water, though there are exceptions. Before fishing for eels in tidal waters, please check with your local Area Fisheries Office.

The Agency has a national rod fishing licence. This means that fishing in all regions is covered by one licence.

Licences are available for coarse fish and non-migratory trout or for all inclusive fishing, including salmon and sea trout.

The licence structure is aimed at raising approximately £14 million for essential fisheries work at a time when the Government's grant-in-aid for this area of the Agency's work is declining.

Coarse fish and non-migratory trout

The price of the full annual licence (1998/99) for coarse fish and non-migratory trout is £16-00 (£8-00 concessions [young anglers aged 12 to 16 years, disabled anglers in receipt of invalidity benefit or severe disability allowance, and anyone aged 65 years and over]).

A short term coarse fish and non-migratory trout licence covers a period of eight consecutive days, giving anglers the benefit of being able to fish over two weekends. This costs £6-00 (no concessions). A one-day licence, aimed at beginners and casual anglers costs £2-00 (no concessions).

Salmon and sea trout

The price of the full annual licence (1998/99) for salmon and sea trout (and also including coarse fish and non-migratory trout) is £55-00 (concessions £27-50). An eight-day licence costs £15-00 and a one-day licence £5-00. There are no concessions on the eight- or one-day licence.

Licences are available from every Post Office in England and Wales or from a range of local distributors. A list of these local distributors is available from the Agency offices. If necessary, you may obtain your licence by post. A form to do this is available from Agency offices.

The 1998/99 licences will be valid until 31 March 1999. Licences are issued on a 12-month basis and are subject to price reviews.

The licence has the following benefits:

* You can use a rod and line anywhere in England and Wales.
* You can use up to two rods per licence, subject to the National Byelaws (see page 13) and any local rules.

Your rod licence will help the Agency to continue and improve the vital work it carries out, including:

* Management of fish stocks
* Surveys, essential for picking up changes and problems.
* Improvements in fisheries and the fish's environment.
* Fish rearing and stocking of rivers.
* Rescue of fish which would otherwise be lost through drought, pollution or other causes.
* Advice on fishing and management issues.
* Protection of stocks through enforcement activities, including anti-poaching patrols.

Please note that:

1. The licence gives you the right to use a fishing rod and line but does not give you the right to fish. You must always check that you have the permission of the owner or tenant of the fishing rights before starting to fish.

2. Your licence is valuable - if it should be

lost, a duplicate can be issued from PO Box 432, National Rod Licence Administration, Environment Agency, Richard Fairclough House, Knutsford Road, Warrington, WA4 1HH. A charge of £5 will be made. Please make a note of the Licence Stamp Number.

3. The licence is yours alone; it cannot be used by anyone else. Please make sure that you sign the licence before you go fishing.

4. Your licence must be produced on demand to a water bailiff of the Agency who produces his or her warrant, a police officer or any other licence holder who produces his or her licence. Failure to do so is an offence and may make you liable to prosecution (maximum fine £2,500).

5. The licence is only valid if the correct name, address and date of birth of the holder, and the date and time of issue are shown without amendments and a stamp of the correct duty is attached and the licence signed by the holder and the issuing agent.

6. A national rod licence is not required where a general licence is in force. Please check with the owner in advance.

7. The catch return form attached to the licence for salmon and sea trout is very important. This information is required by law and you should send in a return, even if you recorded a "nil" catch. Please fill in and return the form in an envelope when your licence expires, using the FREEPOST address.

8. Details of rod fishing byelaws and angling information can be obtained from Agency offices. Fishery byelaws may vary between different Agency Regions - if in doubt, check first. Details of the main byelaws applying to the Agency in the South West can be found on pages 9 to 14.

Salmon and sea trout kelts

Salmon and sea trout which are about to spawn, or have recently spawned but not recovered, are known as unclean. Fish in either condition, if caught, must by law be returned to the water with as little damage as possible. Fish about to spawn are identifiable by the ease with which eggs or milt can be extruded from the vent.

Those having recently spawned are called kelts and can be identified from clean fish by using the comparison given below.

KELT

1. Line of back and belly parallel
2. Gill maggots almost invariably present (salmon only)
3. Distinct "corner" or change of direction in profile of body at back of skull
4. Fins invariably frayed
5. Vent suffused and easily extruded by pressure
6. Belly normally black

CLEAN

1. Back and belly convex in relation to each other
2. Gill maggots only present in previous spawners or fish which have been some time in the river
3. Head tapers into body without a break
4. Fins entire; rarely frayed
5. Vent firm and compact
6. Belly normally pale

Smolts and parr

Young salmon known as parr look very similar to brown trout and are often caught by trout anglers. These parr are destined to run the rivers in a few years as adult salmon after feeding at sea. It is an offence knowingly to take, kill or injure these parr and any which are caught by mistake must be returned to the water.

Salmon parr can be identified from trout by using the comparison given below. In March, April and May, salmon and sea trout parr begin to migrate to the sea. The spots and finger marks disappear and the body becomes silvery in colour. They are then called smolts and must be returned to the water if caught.

SALMON PARR

1. Body slightly built and torpedo-shaped
2. Tail distinctly forked
3. A perpendicular line from the back of the eye will not touch the maxillary bone
4. Eight to twelve finger marks, even in width, well-defined and regularly placed along the sides
5. No white line on leading edge of fins
6. No red colour on adipose fin

TROUT

1. Body thicker and clumsier looking
2. Tail with shallow fork
3. A perpendicular line from the back of the eye will pass through or touch the maxillary bone
4. Finger marks less numerous, uneven in width, less defined, irregularly placed along the sides
5. Normally white line on leading edge of fins
6. Adipose fin generally coloured with orange or red

ROD FISHING SEASONS

The "Open Seasons", i.e. the periods when it is permitted to fish, are set out in the table opposite.

★ *There is no statutory close season for still waters, but some clubs and fishery owners may impose their own close seasons.*

FISHERY DISTRICT	MAJOR RIVERS WITHIN DISTRICT	ROD & LINE OPEN SEASON (dates inclusive)	
SALMON		**Starts**	**Ends**
Avon (Devon)	Avon (Devon)	15 Apr	30 Nov
	Erme	15 Mar	31 Oct
Axe (Devon)	Axe, Otter, Sid	15 Mar	31 Oct
	Lim	1 Mar	30 Sept
Camel	Camel	1 Apr	15 Dec
Dart	Dart	1 Feb	30 Sept
Exe	Exe	14 Feb	30 Sept
Fowey	Fowey, Looe, Seaton	1 Apr	15 Dec
Tamar & Plym	Tamar, Tavy, Lynher,	1 Mar	14 Oct
	Plym, Yealm	1 Apr	15 Dec
Taw & Torridge	Taw, Torridge	1 Mar	30 Sept
	Lyn	1 Feb	31 Oct
Teign	Teign	1 Feb	30 Sept
Frome (Dorset) & Piddle		1 Mar	31 Aug
	All other rivers in North & South Wessex Areas	1 Feb	31 Aug
MIGRATORY TROUT			
Avon (Devon)	Avon (Devon)	15 Apr	30 Sept
	Erme	15 Mar	30 Sept
Axe (Devon)	Axe, Otter, Sid	15 Apr	31 Oct
	Lim	16 Apr	31 Oct
Camel	Camel, Gannel, Menalhyl Valency	1 Apr	30 Sept
Dart	Dart	15 Mar	30 Sept
Exe	Exe	15 Mar	30 Sept
Fowey	Fowey, Looe, Seaton, Tresillian	1 Apr	30 Sept
Tamar & Plym	Tamar, Lynher, Plym, Tavy, Yealm	3 Mar	30 Sept
Taw & Torridge	Taw, Torridge, Lyn	15 Mar	30 Sept
Teign	Teign	15 Mar	30 Sept
	All rivers in North & South Wessex Areas	15 Apr	31 Oct
BROWN TROUT			
	Camel	1 Apr	30 Sept
	Other rivers in Devon & Cornwall Areas	15 Mar	30 Sept
	All rivers in North & South Wessex Areas	1 Apr	15 Oct
	All other water in Devon & Cornwall Areas	15 Mar	12 Oct
	All other waters in North & South Wessex Areas	17 Mar	14 Oct
RAINBOW TROUT			
	Camel & Fowey	1 Apr	30 Sept
	Other rivers in Devon & Cornwall Areas	15 Mar	30 Sept
	All rivers in North & South Wessex Areas	1 Apr	15 Oct
	Reservoirs, Lakes & Ponds	No close season	
GRAYLING, COARSE FISH & EELS			
	Rivers, Streams and Drains. Kennet and Avon Canal Bridgwater & Taunton Canal	16 Jun	14 Mar
	Enclosed waters - Ponds, Lakes & Reservoirs, Exeter Canal, Bude Canal, Great Western Canal.	No close season	

PERMITTED BAITS

The use of particular baits for fishing is regulated by byelaws and in some cases additional restrictions are imposed by the fishing association or riparian owner. The byelaw restrictions are shown in the table:

★ *This restriction only applies to water where a statutory coarse fish close season is applicable. It does not apply to stillwaters.*

★★ *All references to "Trout" include migratory trout and non-migratory trout.*

★★★ *This is a change introduced for the 1998 season.*

No spinning for trout in waters included within the Dartmoor National Park, the Exe above Exebridge, Otter above Langford Bridge, Torridge above Woodford Bridge, Bray above Newton Bridge, Mole above Alswear Bridge, Little Dart above Affeton Bridge, and the whole of the Okement, Lyn and Barnstaple Yeo.

Artificial baits which spin: When fishing for salmon or trout in the Avon (Devon), Axe (Devon), Exe, Dart, Taw and Torridge and Teign districts, use of any artificial bait which spins is restricted to those with only a single, double or treble hook. The width of the hook must not be greater than the spread of the vanes of the bait.

SIZE LIMITS

Length to be measured from tip of the snout to the fork or cleft of the tail.

The size limits, below which fish must be returned, imposed by byelaws are set out in the table. Riparian owners and fishing associations may impose further restrictions which anglers should familiarize themselves with before fishing.

NEW BYELAW FOR TAW/ TORRIDGE

Any salmon taken in August or September on Taw and Torridge which is greater than 70cm in length must be returned. This is one of the new measures to protect spring fish which may become catchable again towards the end of the season. See also **BAG LIMITS** and **PERMITTED BAITS** for other changes.

These size restrictions do not apply to:

(a) Any person who takes any undersized fish unintentionally if he/she at once returns it to the water with as little injury as possible.

(b) Non-migratory trout in any waters included within the Dartmoor National Park, the Exe above Exebridge, the Otter above Langford Bridge, the Torridge above Woodford Bridge, the Mole above Alswear Bridge, the Little Dart above Affeton Bridge and the whole of the Rivers Okement, Lyn and Barnstaple Yeo.

PERMITTED BAITS

FISHERY DISTRICT	SPECIES	BAITS (REAL OR IMITATION)
Avon (Devon)	Salmon & Trout ★★	No worm or maggot.
Axe (Devon)	Salmon & Trout	No shrimp, prawn, worm or maggot. Fly only after 31 July below Axbridge, Colyford.
Dart	Salmon	No worm or maggot. No shrimp or prawn except below Staverton Bridge. No spinning above Holne Bridge.
	Trout	Fly only.
Exe	Salmon & Trout	No worm or maggot.
Barnstaple Yeo (tidal)	All species (inc. sea fish)	No fishing
Taw & Torridge (except Lyn)	Salmon & Trout	No shrimp, prawn, worm or maggot. No spinning after 31 March. ★★★
Lyn	Salmon & Trout	No worm or maggot before 1 June.
Teign	Salmon & Trout	No worm or maggot before 1 June.
Camel & Fowey	Salmon & Trout	No byelaw restrictions on bait.
Tamar	Salmon & Migratory Trout	No worm, maggot, shrimp or prawn after 31 August.
North Wessex & South Wessex Areas	Salmon & Migratory Trout	Artificial fly only before 15 May.
North Wessex & South Wessex Areas	All species in rivers, drains and canals	No maggot (or pupae), processed product, cereal or other vegetable matter during the coarse fish close season. ★

SIZE LIMITS

AREA, DISTRICT OR CATCHMENT	MIGRATORY TROUT	NON-MIGRATORY TROUT	GRAYLING
Camel, Fowey, Tamar and Plym	7 inches	7 inches	N/A
Avon (Devon), Axe (Devon), Dart, Exe, Taw & Torridge, Teign	10 inches	8 inches	N/A
River Lim	N/A	9 inches	N/A
North Wessex (except By Brook)	35 centimetres	25 centimetres	25 centimetres
By Brook & tributaries	35 centimetres	20 centimetres	25 centimetres
South Wessex	35 centimetres	25 centimetres	N/A

MANDATORY BAG LIMITS

North Wessex Area. The bag limits set out in the table below are imposed by the byelaws, however, some riparian owners or angling associations obtain dispensation to increase their bag limits. Anglers should familiarize themselves with bag limits before fishing. Once a bag limit has been taken, the angler may continue fishing for the same species, provided that any fish caught are returned without injury. Freshwater fish other than grayling, pike and eels may not be permanently removed from the water.

RIVER OR AREA	SPECIES	PERIOD		
		24 HOURS	7 DAYS	SEASON
North Wessex	Non-migratory Trout	2	N/A	N/A
	Grayling	2	N/A	N/A

TAW & TORRIDGE

Following a public enquiry in 1997 new bag limits have been imposed for four years, commencing in 1998.

RIVER OR AREA	SPECIES	PERIOD		
		24 HOURS	7 DAYS	SEASON
Taw	Salmon	2	3	10
	Migratory Trout	5	15	40
Torridge	Salmon	2	2	5
		2	7	20

NOTE:

Only two salmon may be killed on each river by an individual angler before 1 June. This measure is specifically designed to protect spring salmon.

VOLUNTARY BAG LIMITS

SPRING SALMON - The Agency is encouraging salmon anglers in Devon and Cornwall, on rivers that have not adopted voluntary measures, to adopt the following bag limits for salmon taken before the beginning of June as follows:

Tavy - one salmon

Lynher, Dart, Teign - two salmon

Salmon anglers on other rivers are asked to show restraint in the early part of the season and are encouraged to fish fly only until the end of May and are asked to return any larger fish, particularly red ones caught later in the season, as these are likely to be multi-sea-winter fish and valuable to the spawning stock. On the rivers Camel, Fowey, Tamar, Exe, Dart and Hampshire Avon a variety of voluntary measures has been adopted to protect fish stocks. Any anglers fishing these rivers should familiarise themselves with these rules before fishing. Details are provided below.

River Camel

The Camel Fisheries Association has agreed limits of two salmon per day and/or four per week. Four sea trout per night, no use of maggots, no fishing in April and no selling of fish.

River Fowey

The Fowey River Association has agreed limits of one salmon per day, two per week and five per season. A day starts at midnight and a week is a rolling period of seven days triggered by the taking of a salmon. Four sea trout may be taken per day, the day commencing at 3.00am. It is strongly recommended that sea trout caught in September be returned.

River Exe

The River Exe and Tributaries Association has agreed that salmon of 28.5" and over in length (9lbs) taken prior to 1 June and all fish of 27.5" and over in length (8lbs) taken after 16 August are to be returned.

River Dart

The Dart Angling Association has agreed to catch and release only to 1 June (appropriate tackle to be used including barbless hooks). After 1 June a limit of two salmon per day and 10 per season. Anglers are encouraged to return any fish greater than 10lb and all coloured, gravid fish. Fly only fishing permitted after taking season bag limit. Sea trout limit two fish per night.

River Tamar

The committee of the River Tamar and Tributaries Fisheries Association has recommended the adoption of a four salmon per-rod-limit before 8 June, one salmon per rod-day from 8 June and any further fish caught to be returned to the water. They further recommend the return of all salmon of 10lb or larger from September 1. However, other voluntary measures may apply on some waters and it is advisable to check details with each owner.

River Hampshire Avon

The Wessex Salmon Association encourages all salmon anglers to practice catch and release in association with the 'swap a salmon' scheme. See page 14 for more details of this scheme on this and other rivers.

CATCH AND RELEASE

With stocks of salmon under increasing pressure, the Environment Agency is seeking to do everything possible to protect the species for the future.

Catch and release is now becoming an established management technique for increasing spawning escapement, particularly where stocks are low. Salmon anglers are encouraged to consider this approach as a means of safeguarding salmon stocks in our rivers.

If you do decide to practice catch and release, the following guidelines may be useful to give your catch the best chance of surviving after you have returned it to the river:

* **Hooks** - single hooks inflict less damage than doubles or trebles, barbless hooks are best. Flatten the barbs on your hooks with pliers.

* **Playing Fish** - fish are best landed before complete exhaustion and therefore all elements of tackle should be strong enough to allow them to be played firmly.

* **Landing Fish** - Fish should be netted and unhooked in the water, if possible. Use knotless nets - not a tailer or gaff.

* **Handling and Unhooking** - Make every effort to keep the fish in the water. Wet your hands. Carefully support the fish out of water. Do not hold the fish up by the tail, this may cause kidney damage. Remove the hook gently - if necessary, cut the line if deeply hooked. Take extra care with spring fish, as they are more susceptible to damage and fungal infection.

Do not under any circumstances keep a fish which is to be returned out of the water for more than 30 seconds. Physiological changes affecting survival begin within one minute.

* **Revive the Fish** - Support an exhausted fish underwater in an upright position facing the current. Estimate weight and length in the water. Avoid weighing. Handle the fish as little as possible. Be patient and give it time to recover and swim away on its own.

HAMPSHIRE AVON - All anglers known to return salmon to the Hampshire Avon will qualify for a Tesco "Swap a Salmon" award. The arrangement, negotiated by the Wessex Salmon Association with Tesco entitles an angler catching and returning a fish to a voucher to be exchanged for a farmed salmon.

FROME AND DART - Similar schemes to the one mentioned above are currently being negotiated for these rivers. Contact your local Fisheries Office for further details.

WILD TROUT SOCIETY - Anglers are asked to return all brown trout caught on the East Dart above Postbridge, on the Cherry Brook and the Blackbrook; while on the West Dart between Blackbrook and Swincombe to return fish between 10" and 16" long.

USE OF OTHER TACKLE

Use of float. The use of a float when fishing for salmon or trout in any waters within the Avon (Devon), Axe (Devon), Dart, Exe, Taw and Torridge, and Teign districts is prohibited.

Use of gaff. See section on national byelaws.

Limit on number of rods in use. See section on national byelaws.

Kilbury Weir. It is illegal to take or attempt to take by any means any fish in any waters within 50 yards below the crest of Kilbury Weir on the River Dart.

Prohibition of use of lead weights. No person shall use any instrument on which is attached directly or indirectly any lead weight (except a weight of 0.06 grams or less, or one of more than 28.35 grams) for the purpose of taking salmon, trout, freshwater fish or eels in any waters within the Agency's region.

LANDING NETS, KEEPNETS AND KEEPSACKS

A new national byelaw has been introduced from 1 April 1998 making it illegal to use landing nets with knotted meshes or meshes of metallic material.

Similarly keepnets should not be constructed of such materials or have holes in the mesh larger than 25mm internal circumference; or be less than 2.0 metres in length. Supporting rings or frames should not be greater than 40cm apart (excluding the distance from the top frame to the first supporting ring or frame) or less than 120cm in circumference.

Keepsacks should be constructed of a soft, dark coloured, non-abrasive, water permeable fabric and should not have dimensions less than 120cm by 90cm if rectangular or; 150cm by 30cm by 40cm if used with a frame or designed with the intention that a frame be used. It is an offence to retain more than one fish in a single keepsack at any time.

The retention of salmonids (adults or juveniles) in keepnets is illegal.

MINIMUM ROD LENGTH

North & South Wessex Areas. No person fishing with rod and line shall use a rod less than 1.5 metres in length (subject to review in phase II of national byelaws).

UNATTENDED RODS

Unattended rods are prohibited for all species in all areas.

THEFT ACT

The Theft Act 1968, Schedule 1, makes it an offence for anyone to take or attempt to take fish in private waters or in a private fishery without the consent of the owner.

The Agency may bring a prosecution under this Act on its own fisheries. It cannot do so on behalf of an individual, and any fishery owner who wishes such a prosecution to be brought should consult the police or a solicitor.

ATTENTION

SALMON AND SEA TROUT ANGLERS Your catch return is needed by 1 January each year. Nil returns are also required. Send returns to:

Environment Agency, FREEPOST, P.O. Box 60, Patchway, Bristol, BS12 4YY.

SEA TROUT

Anglers fishing the Teign, Dart, Tavy, Tamar, Camel and Taw are encouraged to support the national sea trout stock description sampling programme by taking scale samples from any sea trout they catch. Further details and a supply of scale packets are available from the area FER Managers at Bodmin and Exminster.

NATIONAL BYELAWS Phase I

A number of national byelaws has recently been approved. These replace or modify regional byelaws that existed before.

A summary of the new byelaws is given below.

1. The annual close season for fishing for rainbow trout by rod and line in all reservoirs, lakes and ponds has been dispensed with.

2. A close season for brown trout is to be retained on all waters.

3. Use of the gaff is prohibited at all times when fishing for salmon, trout and freshwater fish or freshwater eels.

4. The number of rods that may be used at any time is as follows:

a. One rod when fishing for salmonids in rivers, streams, drains and canals.

b. Two rods when fishing for salmonids in reservoirs, lakes and ponds (subject to local rules).

c. Up to four rods when fishing for coarse fish and eels (subject to local rules).

When fishing with multiple rods and lines, rods shall not be left unattended and shall be placed such that the distance between the butts of the end rods does not exceed three metres.

5. Catch returns for salmon and migratory trout should be submitted no later than 1 January in the following year.

6. See separate section on landing nets, keepnets and keepsacks.

NATIONAL BYELAWS Phase II

A further series of byelaw changes is being considered for introduction in 1999, including: use of crayfish as bait, fishing for crayfish, removal of fish, return of foul hooked fish, removal of fish for use as bait, minimum rod length and unattended rods.

COARSE FISH CLOSE SEASON ON CANALS

In the section on rod fishing seasons it will be seen that canals in Devon and Cornwall are exempt from a close season for coarse fish and eels whereas those in Wessex are not. New proposals dispensing with the close season on most canals are likely to be in place for 1999.

FISH WITH ADIPOSE FINS REMOVED

As indicated on your rod licence, you may catch a fish from which the adipose fin has been completely removed. (These may carry a micro tag implanted within their nose - invisible to you.) If this occurs, you should follow the licence instructions:

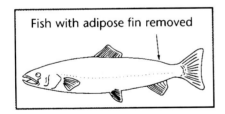

Fish with adipose fin removed

* Dial 100 and ask the operator for FREEPHONE FISHWATCH.
* Tell us your name, address and telephone number.
* Record details of your catch (where, when, size and species of fish).
* Keep the fish (or just the head) frozen if necessary and we will contact you to make arrangements for it to be inspected.

We will pay you a reward if it carries a micro tag and, of course, you keep the fish;

Details should be sent to the appropriate Area Fisheries Office.

PURCHASE AND RELEASE OF SALMON FROM LICENSED NETS

In recent years, the Environment Agency has purchased salmon from the Mudeford nets for release to the Hampshire Avon as extra spawners to help boost stock recovery rates. If suitable arrangements can be made, this will continue in the 1998 season.

These fish will carry a green Floy tag below the dorsal fin and you are particularly requested to practise catch and release of these fish.

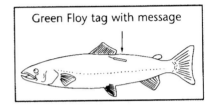

Green Floy tag with message

If you catch such a fish, note the number on the Floy tag, and the estimated length and weight of the fish before releasing it. If you send these details along with the date, time and place of capture to your local Environment Agency Fisheries Officer, you will qualify for a reward of £5 and also a reward under the TESCO "SWAP A SALMON" scheme. You will also help the Agency to gain valuable stock management information.

STOCKING FISH - BUYER BEWARE

In 1996, the Environment Agency brought out a leaflet entitled "Buyer Beware - your guide to stocking fish". The leaflet explains the Agency rules on fish introduction (Section 30, Salmon and Freshwater Fisheries Act 1975) and the common sense things fishery owners can do to protect themselves and their fisheries when buying/stocking fish.

Before introducing (stocking) any fish (or fish spawn) into inland waters, you must obtain written consent of the Agency. Failure to meet this obligation is a criminal offence and could lead to prosecution, with a fine of up to £2,500. In addition, the stocking of non-native species such as Wels Catfish or Grass Carp requires MAFF approval under the Wildlife and Countryside Act 1981.

Mandatory health checks will be required where fish are to be moved into rivers, streams, drains or canals, or where the risk to other fisheries is high.

Health checks will not normally be required in waters where the risk of fish escape is minimal (e.g. enclosed waters). However, there may be occasions where the Agency will still insist on a health examination.

Regardless of the Agency's requirement for health checks, it should be stressed that establishing the health of fish before any stocking is essential. The Agency encourages everyone to follow the Agency's "Buyer Beware" code. Copies of the leaflet can be obtained from any of the Agency's Fisheries Offices.

LOOK OUT! - LOOK UP!
ADVICE ON SAFE FISHING NEAR OVERHEAD ELECTRIC POWER LINES

Several people have died and others have been seriously injured whilst using fishing rods and poles near overhead electric power lines. The following advice is designed to prevent these events recurring:

i   Because rods and poles conduct electricity, they are particularly dangerous when used near overhead electric power lines. Remember that electricity can jump gaps and a rod does not even have to touch an electric line to cause a lethal current to flow.

ii   Many overhead electric power lines are supported by wood poles which can be and are mistaken for telegraph poles. These overhead lines may carry electricity up to 132,000 volts, and have been involved in many of the accidents that have occurred.

iii   The height of high voltage overhead electric power lines can be as low as 5.2 metres and they are therefore within easy reach of a rod or pole. Remember that overhead lines may not be readily visible from the ground. They may be concealed by hedges or by a dark background. Make sure you **"Look Out"** and **"Look Up"** to check for overhead lines before you tackle up and begin fishing.

iv   In general, the minimum safe fishing distance from an overhead electric power line is 30 metres from the overhead line (measured along the ground).

v   When pegging out for matches or competitions, organisers and competitors should, in general, ensure that no peg is nearer to an overhead electric power line than 30 metres (measured along the ground).

vi   For further advice on safe fishing at specific locations please contact your local Electricity Company.

vii   Finally, remember that it is dangerous for any object to get too close to overhead electric power lines, particularly if the object is an electrical conductor, e.g. lead cored fishing line, damp fishing line, rod or pole.

ENVIRONMENT AGENCY AREAS

Devon Area

Fishery Districts (Rivers in parentheses): Avon (Avon, Erme); Axe (Axe, Sid, Otter); Dart (Dart); Exe (Exe); Taw and Torridge (Taw, Torridge, Lyn); Teign (Teign). The River Lim is included in the Devon Area.

Fisheries Officers Tel. (01392) 444000.

Cornwall Area

Fishery Districts (Rivers in parentheses): Camel (Camel, other streams flowing into the sea on the North coast between Marshland Mouth and Lands End); Fowey (Fowey, East and West Looe, Seaton, Tresillian, other streams flowing into the sea on the South coast between Lands End and Rame Head); Tamar and Plym (Tamar, Plym, Tavy and Yealm).

Fisheries Officers Tel. (01208) 78301.

North Wessex Area

River Catchments: Bristol Avon (including all tributaries), Axe (Somerset), Brue, Parrett, Tone, Yeo and all other rivers, drains and streams flowing into the Bristol Channel between Avonmouth and Foreland Point.

Fisheries Officers Tel. (01278) 457333.

South Wessex Area

River Catchments: Hampshire Avon (including all tributaries), Stour (including all tributaries), Dorset Frome, Piddle, Wey, Brit and Char and all other streams flowing into the sea between Christchurch Harbour and Charmouth.

Fisheries Officers Tel. (01258) 456080

ROD LICENCE

IN ORDER TO FISH FOR SALMON, TROUT (INCLUDING MIGRATORY TROUT), FRESHWATER FISH AND EELS IN ANY* WATERS IN THE SOUTH WEST REGION, ANGLERS WILL NEED AN ENVIRONMENT AGENCY NATIONAL ROD LICENCE AND PERMISSION FROM THE OWNER OF THE FISHERY.

ANGLERS MUST CARRY THEIR ROD LICENCES WITH THEM AT ALL TIMES WHILE FISHING.

* Except in waters where a General Licence is in force - please check with the owner of the fishery in advance.

ENVIRONMENT AGENCY

Wild Trout in the South West

Mike Weaver

stop rising at the slightest ripple from your wading, and quite often they are feeding on some minute item that is almost impossible to match with an artificial fly.

What, however, can match the excitement of wading up a moorland stream, casting your fly into every little pool between the cascades, or crouching by a meandering meadow stream as the browns suck in the mayflies. The trout may be of modest size but when they come to the net you are often staggered by the beauty of what you have caught. And the problems of these moody, spooky and just plain difficult fish are really the challenges that so many anglers are seeking. Yes, you have to put in your apprenticeship to be consistently successful with wild trout, but success when it comes more than repays the effort.

Thanks to the dramatic growth of stocked reservoirs and purpose-built trout lakes, trout fishing is now more widely available than ever before and these new fisheries have provided countless thousands of anglers with the opportunity to cast a fly for trout without travelling far from home.

This expansion of stillwater trout fishing, however, has come at a time which has also seen a decline in stocks of our native wild brown trout in many areas.

Fortunately, there are parts of this crowded island where it is still possible to enjoy a truly wild experience, fishing up a moorland river or a meadow stream for brown trout that have never seen a hatchery, and the south west of England provides endless opportunities for searching out the wild trout.

So, what's so special about wild trout. In the south west it rarely if ever grows to the sizes that are little more than average on lakes and reservoirs. Wild trout are often as moody as the weather, they scatter in all directions at the first wave of your rod or

So where can the visitor fish for those wild browns of the south west? The moors are the logical starting point and the biggest of these is Dartmoor, often called the last wilderness in southern England. Many of Devon's major rivers like the Dart, Teign, Tavy and Taw spring to life on Dartmoor and their upper reaches and tributaries provide many miles of moorland trout fishing. Virtually all of the Dart system above Dartmeet, where the East and West Dart join, is Duchy of Cornwall water and a modestly-priced day permit presents you with more than 25 miles of varied fishing. Not only does this permit include the East and West Dart but also the fascinating little tributaries - Cherry Brook, Swincombe, Wallabrook, Cowsic and Blackbrook.

On the western edge of Dartmoor, miles of trout fishing on the Tavy, Walkham, Plym and Meavy can be fished with a Tavy Walkham & Plym Fishing Club permit, and the wooded valley of the upper reaches of the Teign on the eastern slopes are available through the Upper Teign Fishing Association.

Game

19lb rainbow caught in the summer of '97.
Valley Springs

Exmoor too offers wild trout fishing in spectacular scenery and nowhere more so than on the East Lyn. From Brendon down to the sea at Lynmouth, the Environment Agency manages the Glenthorne and Watersmeet fisheries, which are full of free-rising colourful trout. Cross to the other side of the moor and you find similar fishing on the Barle at the Tarr Steps Hotel, with a long stretch of water above and below the much-visited clapper bridge. The visitor can fish more of the Barle, as well as the upper Exe, downstream at the Carnarvon Arms Hotel near Dulverton.

Bodmin Moor is the south west's other moorland area but here the upper reaches of the Fowey and Camel are looked upon primarily as spawning and nursery areas for salmon, with little trout fishing available.

Down from the moors there are many more opportunities to go in search of wild trout.

Many anglers who fish for salmon on the middle and lower reaches of major rivers like the Exe, Taw, Torridge or Tamar will often have their flies or spinners seized by good-sized brown trout. This is no fluke as these rivers often hold surprisingly large stocks of trout which are rarely fished for and an outing with the dry fly in May and June, or a summer evening when the sedges and sherry spinners are on the water, can provide a pleasant surprise.

Some of the most enhancing fishing of all is on the small lowland tributaries of the big rivers. These streams, often little more than brooks, provide really intimate fly fishing as they meander through the meadows and respond well to both dry fly and nymph fishing. The accumulation of silt on the bottom of these quiet streams provides an ideal habitat for the larvae of the mayfly and a hatch of this big insect at the end of May or the beginning of June can be the highlight of the season. Many anglers in search of this kind of fishing visit the Arundell Arms at Lifton where the Lyd, Thrushel, Wolf, Lew, Carey and Ottery offer miles of small-stream fly fishing.

The manicured chalk streams of Wessex, in spite of a century of stocking, offer more wild trout fishing than you may think. For more than a dozen years, the Wessex Fly Fishing waters on the Piddle at Tolpuddle in Dorset have operated on a catch-and-release basis and many other stretches of chalk stream in Dorset and Wiltshire are now being managed to reduce the dependence on constant stocking, thus providing exciting fishing and reducing costs.

So, there is plenty of wild trout fishing to be found in the south west at a very reasonable price, but this treasure can only be kept intact by adopting the right conservation measures. In the past, the response to declining stocks was to order another truckload of trout from the hatchery. Now, anglers and fishery managers are increasingly turning to habitat improvement and reducing the number of trout killed. More and more fly fishers are returning their wild browns to the river and paying a visit to the nearest stocked lake when they need to fill the freezer.

For 1998, a new voluntary scheme has come into operation on four stretches of the Duchy of Cornwall fishery on Dartmoor. The Wild Trout Society and the Duchy of Cornwall are asking anglers to return trout on the upper East Dart, Cherry Brook, Blackbrook and a stretch of the West Dart in an effort to increase the number of the bigger fish that anglers enjoy catching. At Amesbury in Wiltshire, another scheme co-ordinated by the Wild Trout Society has restored a degraded stretch of the Avon to re-create the natural sequence of meanders, pools and riffles that wild trout need to prosper.

These and other projects show how anglers in co-operation with the Environment Agency can make a real contribution towards protecting and enhancing the stocks of wild trout in the rivers of the south west.

If you wish to find out more about the Wild Trout Society, send for details to The Wild Trout Society, PO Box 2903, Dorchester, DT2 7DX.

What is the Salmon & Trout Association?

Formed in 1903 by the Worshipful Company of Fishmongers in the City of London, the Salmon & Trout Association (S&TA) is the only UK-wide organisation representing the views of game anglers. S&TA has been an independent organisation since 1973, with offices in London and Edinburgh.

A membership of 15,000 individuals and 300 clubs means we support around 100,000 game anglers in England, Scotland, Wales and Northern Ireland. 52 branches across the UK provide a social focus for members and allow local issues to be closely monitored. 8 Regional Chairmen coordinate branches in their areas and bring issues to S&TA Council for national action.

S&TA represents the interests of all game anglers, the species for which they fish and the environment in which those species are found:

* Migratory salmon and sea trout
* Wild brown trout and grayling
* Rainbow trout in stillwaters

S&TA has three main strands to its brief:
* Political power in Parliament
* Education
* Conservation of the aquatic environment

POLITICAL POWER IN PARLIAMENT

S&TA is primarily a political lobbying organisation on behalf of game anglers. 80 members across both Houses of Parliament give us genuine influence when decisions concerning the future of our sport are taken. We have close liaison with Government Departments and Agencies:

Environment Agency - the regulatory body for fisheries in England and Wales. We influence such issues as licence fees, water resources, the regulation of migratory fish exploitation and the drafting of new by-laws

Scottish Environment Protection Agency (SEPA) - increasingly influential in Scotland, and a potential ally in the independent regulation of fish farming

Ministry of Agriculture, Fisheries & Food (MAFF) - the Government has promised a review of the Salmon & Freshwater Fisheries Act and S&TA has set up a working party to review the Act with the full cooperation of MAFF

All aspects of our work are bedevilled by outdated legislation and this is the most important part of our work over the next five years

Scottish Office - responsible for fisheries in Scotland. S&TA lobby directly on relevant matters

European Parliament - increasingly important in relevant legislation, particularly concerning predator control and industrial fishing. S&TA have direct lobbying influence through the European Anglers Alliance

United Voice for Angling - S&TA is playing a major role in bringing all UK anglers under a single umbrella organisation to speak with one voice for our sport to both Government Agencies and Sports Council

EDUCATION

Education is a high priority with S&TA, particularly in bringing the young into the sport and we have run a Junior Beginners' Course on the Wiltshire Avon for 27 years. Branches organise local tuition days and S&TA now has a national programme of education which encompasses the following policy:

No child should be excluded from tuition days on the grounds of cost

All S&TA tuition is carried out by qualified instructors. Tuition days are spread across the UK so that all children have the opportunity of participating in an event in their area

Funding - S&TA looks to funding for our Education Programme through the Sports Council and the Salmon & Trout Trust, with whom we have a close association

Qualified Instruction - S&TA has its own

Game

Superb brown of exactly 10lb for Benny Jones of Torrington. Stafford Moor

professional qualification - S&TA National Instructors' Certificate (STANIC) - and works closely with the other professional Instructors' bodies, APGAI and REFFIS

CONSERVATION OF THE AQUATIC ENVIRONMENT

Water Resources - each S&TA branch has a Water Resources Officer who monitors all local abstraction and discharge licenses. S&TA's Water Resources Committee lobbys Government Departments and Agencies on all relevant water resource matters and takes an active advisory role in research projects

Salmon & Trout Trust - this charitable Trust is closely associated with S&TA and provides finance for various projects:

Wild brown trout habitat restoration on Wiltshire Avon by supporting Game Conservancy work

Wild brown trout parasite infestation in Highland loch populations

Effects of barley straw on algal blooms in rivers

Impact of introduced coarse fish species on wild salmonid populations in Loch Lomond

Education - support of S&TA's youth education programme

Annual Scholarship to a King's College MSc Fisheries student

Other conservation bodies - S&TA works closely on relevant issues with many conservation bodies, including WWF, Greenpeace, RSPB, Game Conservancy, Grayling Society and Wild Trout Society

CURRENT ISSUES

Fisheries Legislation - the most important part of our lobbying work. S&TA will be undertaking a review of the Salmon & Freshwater Fisheries Act with the full cooperation of MAFF

Commercial salmon netting - S&TA continues to lobby for an end to all commercial netting for salmon and sea trout on the grounds of stock management and the socio-economic importance of angling

Sea Trout Collapse - S&TA has combined with SANA in Scotland to form a Sea Trout Group to lobby the Scottish Office against the harmful effects of fish farming on sea trout stocks

Predation - S&TA has taken a leading role in the fight for effective, responsible management plans to control cormorants and sawbill ducks in both the UK and Europe. We are also pressing for non-lethal management of the increasing seal population around the coast of Scotland

Afforestation & Acidification - changes in the catchment environment affecting the spawning and survival of salmonids

Spring salmon - We are pressing MAFF and the Environment Agency to protect spring salmon stocks by postponing the netting season until June 1st. We also advocate angler restraint to protect this vulnerable stock

Abstraction - a serious threat to many rivers throughout the UK. We are heavily involved in lobbying and research

Industrial fishing - a huge industry threatening the food chain and migrating salmonid smolts which are taken as a by-catch of the fishery. S&TA has joined forces with Greenpeace, WWF, RSPB and others in the Marine Stewardship Council, bringing public awareness to this problem and enormous political influence

Antis - S&TA keeps the future of our sport at the centre of our lobbying policy, including speaking regularly with relevant politicians in all three major parties

Funding for Angling Education - S&TA has led the fight to change the Sports Council's attitude towards angling and support us with the sort of funding a participation sport of our size deserves

MEMBERS' BENEFITS

No angler could ask for a better package of benefits and they are free to members:
* £2m Public Liability Insurance
* Discounts on fishing products
* Money off stillwater fishery permits
* Bargain fishing holidays
* Special rates on tackle insurance
* Reduction on public health care
* Reduced car insurance
* Special Affinity credit card

Local contact details are on page 52.

Game

*10lb sea trout on a fly for Tyson Jackson.
Butterwell Fishery - River Camel*

25

Peninsula Fisheries

Peninsula Fisheries is a part of South West Water's Leisure Services department which looks after thousands of acres of land and water in the South West of England. As well as countryside management and 29 fisheries, its interest extends to Watersports Centres, Cafeterias and Gift Shops.

Since 1989 Leisure Services has run its fishing and other business as stand alone activities. This means that anglers pay for their own sport without any subsidy.

This self supporting policy has meant that we have been able to gradually improve our facilities and product which we offer. Average stock size on our Premier Rainbow fisheries has increased to 2lb. Not only does this give extra value for money but helps to reduce cormorant predation.

We have been able to keep prices this year at '97 levels apart from a slight increase for boats and season permits on our Low Cost Fisheries. Our prices have been slashed at Roadford to encourage anglers to try this Premier Brown Trout water.

We are changing our entire boat fleet and using traditional style boats in the Bonwitco range. Another 5 new boats at Wimbleball this year will be added to the 5 in 1997. The Kennick fleet is next in line for 1999.

Our self service kiosks and interpretation have been upgraded making them more inviting and informative.

Another initiative on the Game fishing front for 1998 is the new Loyalty Card for regular Peninsula anglers. 6 visits over a two month period gives the 7th FREE.

Our South West Water organised fly fishing competition 'The Classic', open to all anglers, is to be held at Siblyback Lake on the 10th May. With no bag limit it will be attractive to the best anglers in the Westcountry. A new Brown Trout boat only fishery will be open at Tottiford to complete an angling package on offer with Kennick the premier rainbow fishery and Trenchford the pike fishery, all within walking distance of each other.

The success of our game fisheries is matched by the 13 Coarse Fisheries we manage. Once again the 100 peg Porth and the 150 peg Upper Tamar are the top competition venues. Most local clubs and leagues use these venues for matches and festivals. Our other coarse lakes supply a complete range to satisfy the pleasure and specimen hunters.

As a result of huge demand we are holding 'The Challenge' a new 150 peg coarse angling competition for individuals both local and national. It will be on the 3rd May at Upper Tamar. Later in the year, on the 30th August, 'The Premier' team event takes place at Tamar for the 3rd year running.

Peninsula Fisheries is the largest supplier of Coarse and Game fishing on the largest waters in the South West and as such has its unique problems. At our Argal Premier fishery during 1997 we saw a serious outbreak of Argulus foliacious (fish lice) which infected the Rainbow stock. The infection was monitored by a fishing exercise in February this year and as a result Argal has closed for the foreseeable future. Because Argal is 65 acres and a supply reservoir, treatment of the fish is virtually impossible.

They say in every cloud there is a 'silver lining'. We have decided to upgrade Siblyback to its former status of a Premier Fishery. This is the 'silver lining' for anglers in south east Cornwall and the Plymouth area. The lake is being heavily stocked with rainbows averaging 2lb and this will put it on a par with Kennick and Wimbleball.

We will continue to strive to give good value for money and excellent customer care and facilities. This is the Peninsula Fisheries mission.

Peninsula Fisheries have established a Peninsula Coarse Angling Association and become a full member of the National Federation of Anglers. It is hoped regular Peninsula anglers will become members of the association.

For information and applications contact Reg England on 01837 871565

PENINSULA FISHERIES TROUT FISHING

STOCKED RAINBOW TROUT

KENNICK - Nr Christow, Devon.
Permits: Self Service Kiosk
Season: 28 March - 31 October
Best Flies: Black Gnat/Montana/Damsel Fly
Biggest Fish 1997: 10lb 14oz Rainbow.
Information: (01837) 871565

WIMBLEBALL LAKE - Nr Dulverton, Somerset.
Permits: Self Service at Hill Farm Barn
Season: 28 March - 31 October
Best Flies: Montana/Soldier Palmer/Buzzer.
Biggest Fish: 10lb 12oz Rainbow.
Information: Office hours (01398) 371372

SIBLYBACK LAKE - Nr Liskeard, Cornwall.
Permits: Self Service Kiosk at Watersports Centre
Season: 28 March - 31 October
Best Flies: Viva/Black & Peacock/Montana
Information: Ranger (01579) 342366

ARGAL - Nr Penryn, Cornwall.
Closed for the forseeable future

BROWN TROUT FISHING

ROADFORD - Nr Okehampton, Devon.
Permits: Angling and Watersports Centre at Lower Goodacre.
Season: 23 March - 12 October
Biggest Fish: 5lb 7oz Brown.
Information: (01409) 211507

COLLIFORD LAKE - Nr Bodmin, Cornwall.
Permits: Jamaica Inn off A30 at Bolventor
Season: 15 March - 12 October
Information: Ranger (01579) 342366

FERNWORTHY LAKE - Nr Chagford, Devon.
Permits: Self Service Kiosk
Season: 1 May - 12 October
Best Flies: Black Gnat/Invicta/G&H Sedge
Information: (01837) 871335

TOTTIFORD - Nr Christow, Devon
BOAT ONLY
Permits: Kennick self service
Season: 15 March - 12 October
Information: (01837) 871565

LOW COST "NATURAL" TROUT FISHING

BURRATOR - Nr Yelverton, Devon.
Permits: The Burrator Inn, Dousland (01822) 853121. Esso Garage, Yelverton.
Season: 15 March - 12 October
Information: Ranger (01837) 871335

STITHIANS - Nr Redruth, Cornwall.
Permits:
Stithians Watersports Centre (01209) 860301.
Londis Supply Store, Stithians (01209) 860409.
Season: 15 March - 12 October
Information: Ranger (01579) 34266

CROWDY RESERVOIR - Nr Camelford, Cornwall.
Permits:
The Spar Shop, Camelford (01840) 212356
Season: 15 March - 12 October
Information: Ranger (01409) 311507

WISTLANDPOUND - Nr Sth Molton, Devon.
Permits: Post Office in Challacombe (01598) 763229.
The Kingfisher, Barnstaple (01271) 344919.
Camera & Picture, Combe Martin (01271) 883275. Variety Sports, Ilfracombe (01271) 862039.
Season: 15 March - 12 October
Information: Ranger (01288) 321262

LOWER TAMAR LAKE - Nr Bude, Cornwall.
Permits: Self Service Kiosk
Season: 15 March - 12 October
Information: Ranger (01288) 321262

FREE TROUT FISHING

MELDON - Nr Okehampton, Devon.
Free to holders of a valid E.A. Rod Licence and is zoned into spinning, bait and fly.
Season: 15 March - 12 October

AVON DAM - South Brent, Devon.
Angling by spinning, fly or bait and is free to valid E.A. licence holders.
Season: 15 March - 12 October

VENFORD - Nr Ashburton, Devon.
Free to holders of valid E.A. Rod Licence and can be fished by spinning, bubble float and bait.
Season: 15 March - 12 October.

Grayling in the South West

By David Pilkington

The grayling, in the past often maligned as vermin on trout rivers, is at last being recognised as a truly sporting and wild fish.

The fact that their season continues after the close of trout fishing, and that they take a fly readily, reinforces their attraction to the thinking, sporting angler.

A surge of interest has taken place in recent years, starting slowly back in the 1970's with the publication of Reg Righyni's classic book 'Grayling', and the formation of the Grayling Society, and continues to gather momentum today, as ever more fishermen pursue this most attractive and elegant fish.

Distribution in the South West

The Wessex region is home to some fine grayling, with the Wiltshire/Hampshire Avon system probably having the densest population in Britain. The Frome holds some very large fish, certainly in the 3lb class, mostly downstream of Dorchester. I believe there are grayling in the Tone, then moving west into Devon and Cornwall we have two isolated but thriving populations in the Exe and Tamar systems. On the Exe they can be found all the way up from Exeter to the Barle junction and into the lowest pools on the Barle. On the Tamar they are well distributed throughout the main river and most of the tributaries, particularly the Inny, Lyd and Ottery. In was on the upper reaches of the Inny, on a cold, grey day in March 1967, that I saw my very first grayling, and I have been fascinated ever since by "The lady of the stream".

Tackle

A light, crisp actioned fly rod of around 9 feet, matched with a floating line no heavier than AFTM 5, is perfect for most waters. I prefer a double tapered line, it allows a more delicate presentation and is more suited to roll casting, often essential on small streams. The reel should be a light no-nonsense job, well filled with line and backing, not for playing the fish but to minimise line coil and memory. I needle knot a 9ft knotless tapered leader (3lb of 5x) and add 3 feet of 2lb nylon as a tippett, attached with a three turn water knot. Waders are useful, with chest waders preferred. You will need all the other accessories you would normally carry when trouting, floatant, sinkant etc. Most essential though is a pair of long nosed forceps of similar to facilitate unhooking and returning your fish. Hooks should be barbless, I often catch salmon parr, unseasonable trout and even sea trout whilst fishing for grayling.

Tactics

First, find your fish! On the clear waters of the Wessex trout streams careful observation with polaroids will soon reveal the fish. Grey shadows on the river bed, ever on the move to intercept a drifting nymph or lumbering caddis. Rising fish are on obvious give away, but are they grayling? or perhaps brown trout or salmon parr. The rise of a grayling can be seen to be slightly different to other game fish, due to the grayling's unique habit of lying hard on the river bed and rising almost vertically to the surface to engulf it's prey, and returning at once to the gravel. This causes the fish to make an oily, kidney shaped whorl on the surface of the water, often accompanied by a bubble as it turns a sort of somersault on it's way back to the river bed. In clear water the fish can often be seen emerging from the depths like a missile a split second before breaking the surface. In the absence of fly hatches and rising fish the only way to find your grayling is to fish all the likely looking areas and, once a fish has been landed, cover the area thoroughly as grayling often shoal. As the trout season ends and the water temperature drops this shoaling behaviour becomes more apparent, with some parts of the river completely devoid of fish, so it pays to know the sort of water the grayling prefer. Local advice and information can be invaluable,

Game

Fishery record brace of rainbows for Mark Hughes from Mid Wales - 31lb 11oz Bellbrook Valley

but if none is available look for steady, even flowing water of between 18 inches and 6 feet in depth, the colder the water the deeper the fish will be.

Wet and Dry Fly

Small wet trout flies, fished either up or downstream will take grayling in summer and early autumn, but are indiscriminate and far less efficient than dry fly or nymph.

A hatch of naturals, in any month of the year will bring grayling to the surface and provide superlative sport on a dry fly. The grayling is a fussy feeder and any untidy presentation will result in the fly being refused. From it's position on the river bed the grayling has a wide field of view, so the fly should land without disturbing the water and drift for several feet without dragging, in order to deceive her ladyship.

Fly patterns are less important than presentation, though if the insect on the water can be identified and matched by a suitable artificial, so much the better. Grayling will often feed on tiny flies and your box should contain a selection from size 12 down to 18 or 20. Despite taking tiny flies it is not unusual to catch grayling while spinning for salmon with a small Mepps and my biggest grayling, a two pounder, took a large lure at night while I was after sea trout! Many of the traditional grayling flies are still highly successful today. Fancy patterns such as Red Tag, Treacle Parkin and Bradshaw's Fancy are excellent. The modern range of cul-de-canard flies, with their highly imitative properties, are very hard to beat. The flies visibility to the angler is also very important, particularly in the fading light of and October or November afternoon. I like parachute style flies with a highly visible wing post of white calf tail or synthetic wool,

the American elk hair caddis is also highly visible and can be very effective, even when caddis flies are absent. Grayling take a fly very quickly and your strike must be equally rapid if you are to hook your fish.

Nymph Fishing

There will, of course, be times when there are no naturals hatching and the surface of the river slides past unbroken by the rings of rising fish. Now is the time for the nymph, without doubt the most effective way of catching grayling. The late Frank Sawyer, river keeper on the officer's club water on the Wiltshire Avon at Netheravon, invented his famous killer bug purely as a way of catching and removing unwanted grayling from a trout fishery. On the chalk streams where the clear water allows fish to be stalked and targeted, cast your weighted nymph upstream of the fish and allow it to drift downstream, keeping an eagle eye on the point where your leader penetrates the surface film. It pays to grease the leader down to the tippet knot and sink the tippet with fullers earth. When the fish takes the knot will twitch or be pulled under and your strike must be instantaneous. If a fish keeps refusing your fly try the 'induced take' by

Game

The 1997 season's best rainbow, a perfectly conditioned 13lb 8oz landed by Henry Gliddon of Exeter. Stafford Moor

lifting the rod just before the nymph reaches the fish. This lifts the nymph enticingly just in front of the fish's nose and few grayling can resist it.

When the fish are not visible I use an indicator on the leader, either a tuft of wool treated with floatant or a pea-sized lump of Float-do or similar material. The position of the indicator determines the depth at which the nymph will fish and, crucially, indicates the take. Obviously a heavy nymph is needed to fish deep water and I am a great fan of the bead headed types. Gold and copper heads work well on most patterns such as hare's ear, pheasant tail and even the original killer bug.

Caution and Conservation

Grayling share their habitat with trout and salmon which spawn during the autumn months. CHECK with the owners of the fishery to see whether fishing for grayling is allowed after the close of the salmon and trout seasons. More importantly, if you can fish, DO NOT WADE anywhere near the pool tails between October and March. Fertile trout and salmon eggs will be buried in the gravel shallows and walking on them will damage our fish stocks for future years.

I would like to close with a word on conservation. At one time grayling were ruthlessly culled from trout streams by any means possible. This has been proven an ineffective as a way of reducing numbers and just reduces the average size of fish. Today most fisheries value the presence of grayling, they are an excellent indication of good water quality and happily co-exist with other game fish. In early autumn, when in their prime, grayling make excellent eating, but only take what you need (they are protected by law through the coarse fish close season, 16 March to 15 June inclusive and other bylaws may apply).

All out truly wild fish stocks are under threat these days and it would be nice to see anglers actively caring for the grayling and the rivers they inhabit.

Classic fly caught 11lb 8oz springer for Chris Marwood.
Wadebridge A.A. water on the River Camel

Pleased with a nice rainbow.
Amherst Lodge

Game

Two brace including a nice brownie for Derek England of Plympton. Mill Leat, Ermington

Fishing with Wessex Water

Whether you are a keen angler, enjoy walking in the countryside or bird spotting, Wessex Water has various recreational facilities at its reservoirs in Somerset and Dorset.

For anglers the fisheries at Clatworthy, Hawkridge and Sutton Bingham reservoirs offer a friendly personal service in picturesque surroundings, while the Durleigh reservoir just south of Bridgwater, provides coarse anglers with a similar opportunity.

The sport at all the Wessex Water reservoirs has received the stamp of approval from one of the county's top anglers. Former England fly fishing captain Chris Ogborne describes the reservoirs as 'a natural haven of peace and solitude.' 'Fishing still matters to me, but of equal importance are the binoculars round my neck and the walking boots on my feet. The lakes are places of retreat - just being there is enough to recharge your batteries,' he said.

SUTTON BINGHAM

This 142 acre reservoir is a lowland fishery on the Somerset and Dorset border situated four miles south of Yeovil. It offers excellent fly fishing for rainbow or brown trout, from March 21 to October 18. Tuition and tackle are available by appointment from the ranger and a fishing lodge has been designed to cater for the disabled.

For more details about fishing contact ranger Ivan Tinsley on 01935 872389.

CLATWORTHY

Situated in the Brendon Hills this 130 acre reservoir provides a picturesque setting for fishing, where the season is from March 21 to October 18, and for walking. Anglers can enjoy fishing for rainbow and brown trout. There are seven water hotspots for fishermen but generally the south bank is considered to be the best area. The fishing

lodge was refurbished in 1997 and now has facilities for the disabled Contact ranger Dave Pursey on 01984 624658 for more information on fishing.

DURLEIGH

This 80 acre lowland reservoir is one of the oldest in the Wessex Water region and was formerly a trout fishery. It is open every day of the year except Christmas Day, Boxing Day and New Year's Day. It is the only Wessex Water reservoir dedicated to the public for coarse fishing and can offer superb fishing for matches or the casual angler. The reservoir contains carp, roach, bream, perch, tench and specimen size pike.

Contact ranger Paul Martin for details about fishing or matches on 01278 424786.

HAWKRIDGE

This 32 acre Upland reservoir nestled in the Quantock Hills is open for fishing between March 28 and November 22.

It provides facilities for brown or rainbow trout from the bank or the boat - anglers are recommended to book boats.

Contact ranger Gary Howe for details about fishing on 01278 455400.

OTTERHEAD LAKES

The two lakes, situated on the Blackdown Hills, south of Taunton are now a nature reserve manged by the Somerset Wildlife Trust. These will be used as a syndicated fishery for trout in 1998 and no public fishing is permitted this year.

TUCKING MILL

This is located in the attractive Midford Valley, south of Bath and runs a season from June 16 1998 to March 14 1999. Wessex Water offers free fishing for disabled anglers at this small water storage lake which is stocked with roach, chub, tench and large carp.

The site is regularly used by disabled angling clubs and there are six specially designed wheelchair platforms with space for two wheelchairs plus further platforms for more mobile anglers.

continues on page 36

Game

Dennis Dawson of Bodmin with a '97 fishery best brown of 12lb 2oz in a three fish bag of 17lb 10oz. Temple Trout

BLASHFORD LAKES

These are a series of working and worked out gravel pits set in the River Avon Valley on the Wiltshire and Hampshire borders.

Blashford and Ivy lakes offer coarse fishing to members of the Christchurch Angling Club during the coarse fishing season. For further information contact club secretary Mr R Andrews on 01425 638502.

1998 PRICE GUIDE

TROUT

Season ticket £360
Season concession £260
valid for one site only seven days per week (excluding Hawkridge winter season)
Dayticket £12
Day concession £10
Evening ticket £7 (no concessions)
Book of tickets £120 for 11 available only from ranger
Book of tickets (concession) £100 for 11
(Book tickets are valid at all Wessex Water reservoirs)
Boat (rowing) £10 per day per boat
Boat (evening) £6
Bag limits: season tickets 4, day permit 5, evening permit 2

COARSE FISHING

Day ticket £4.50
Day concession £3
Evening ticket £3
Book of tickets £30 for 10

Rod Review

by Roddy Rae - Professional Fly Fishing Instructor. REFFIS & STANIC

Bruce & Walker Speycasters

There are many rod makers who produce quality fly rods but none, in my opinion, that can match Bruce & Walker for being at the forefront of salmon rod design.

Their range of Powerlight Speycasters offer the discerning salmon angler a choice of lengths and actions that will suit any conditions that British rivers will throw at him.

After field testing these rods over two seasons and comparing them to many other makes, the Speycasters come out in front by yards.

The 12'4" rated for lines 8/9 is, I feel, the ideal rod for most situations in the west country. It's lightness and power will speycast 30 yards of line with ease, handling floating and sinking lines admirably.

Rod specification is: matt dark mahogany blank, wine whippings with gold tipping. Hard, high stand off snake chrome rings. The rod has a deluxe rosewood reel seat with hand crafted down locking fine thread secure fitting, which will take all types of reels. It has a traditional aluminium end cap with a rubber button and comes complete with a partitioned rod bag.

All the rods come with a lifetime guarantee against manufacturing faults.

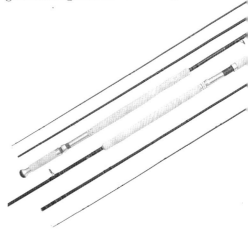

Game

Largest rainbow of 1997 at 12lb 5oz for Graham Bray of St Austell.
Temple Trout

37

▬BRISTOL▬
WATER
fisheries

CHEW VALLEY LAKE
BLAGDON LAKE
THE BARROWS

For the best fly fishing in the West, come and try the Bristol Water fisheries, in beautiful Mendip country, just south of Bristol.

The first reservoir to offer public fishing for grown-on stillwater trout was our Blagdon Lake in the year 1904. Today our large lake fisheries continue to offer exciting sport in lovely surroundings and our Lodges and friendly staff offer the best of modern facilities combined with old world courtesy.

CHEW, at 1,200 acres, is our largest lake and it lies some seven miles due south of Bristol. It is most renowned for loch style boat fishing and is a centre of excellence for the talented competition anglers from all over the West Country.

There are 31 boats, each equipped with an outboard motor, and plenty of room on the lake for expert and pleasure anglers alike. May and June are the best months when a variety of buzzers hatch and bring the trout to the surface. Casting to rising fish and hooking and playing our superb quality, hard fighting rainbows, which average over 2lbs, is the pinnacle of stillwater fly fishing.

Bank fishing is best early and late in the season and provides a chance to explore many miles of uncrowded lake margin. The extended season bank fishing for rainbows was very popular last year, with excellent catches at reduced permit prices. As a result we will again stay open till late November this year.

BLAGDON LAKE is 440 acres and has 16 rowing boats. A number of anglers use their own electric outboard motors but with no noisy petrol engines the fishery is more peaceful than Chew. Boat fishing is similar to that at Chew, though there are fewer buzzers and more sedges and damsel nymphs to bring the trout to the surface.

The bank fishing is good, particularly in April/May and again in September/October. There are many bank hotspots and at all of them you will find ample space to fish in lovely surroundings with Cowslips and Purple Orchids underfoot, Buzzards wheeling overhead and Swallows competing with the trout for the hatching flies.

THE BARROWS.~. These three reservoirs of 60, 40 and 25 acres were built late in the last Century. They are bank only fisheries and are stocked with slightly smaller trout, but perhaps provide the most reliable bank sport of all our lakes. No 1 reservoir is brown trout only and No 2 rainbow only, while No 3 contains a mixture. Evening fishing can be particularly good as buzzers and sedges hatch to give exciting rises.

On 4 and 5 July 1998 we will allow float tube fishing as a trial. There should be equipment for hire so come along if you fancy a go at this novel means of fly fishing.

Game

On the lookout for a fish at Innis Country Club

Our Lodges. The centre for bookings, enquiries, Permits and most tackle sales is Woodford Lodge at Chew Lake. This offers a comfortable lounge where anglers can have a full breakfast before the day's fishing, and find out about the best tactics and current most productive areas. There is a drying room for wet clothes, pay telephone, drinks machine and, of course, lavatories and wash rooms. The Lodge is accessible to wheelchairs.

At Blagdon our half-timbered lodge offers similar facilities, but is smaller than Woodford, and at the Barrows there is a self-service kiosk for permits and separate lavatories and shelters.

Our Day Bank Permits cost £13 at Blagdon, £11 at Chew and £9 at the Barrows, with concessions and afternoon/evening Permits from 1 May.

Boat Permits are £21 per person at Blagdon and £26.50 at Chew. The limit is 8 trout for all Day Permits.

In August, when you buy a Bank Permit or a Chew Boat Permit, you get another one FREE.

Youth Competition. On Tuesday 26 May we will hold our third Youth Competition.

Open to all young anglers between 12 and 19 years, this is a boat competition at Chew, with ghillies, and over £800 worth of prizes on offer. The entrance fee of £12.50 includes Permits and an evening buffet. Details and booking forms may be obtained from Woodford Lodge.

Tuition. We run two very popular Beginners' Days, on 25 April and 17 May, and regular casting and full tuition courses. At the top end of the market England International, John Horsey, also offers expert tuition in loch style boat fishing at Chew or Blagdon.

1998 Season. Runs from 26 March to 29 November.

Phone or write to Bristol Water Fisheries, Woodford Lodge, Chew Stoke, Bristol BS40 8XH. Telephone/Fax: 01275 332339 for a free 1998 Brochure and for enquiries or boat bookings

Stillwater Trout Fishing in Wessex

by Dave Cooling

As with the coarse fishing, the stillwater trout scene in Wessex can be neatly divided along the geological boundary of the chalk, but perhaps with even more distinct differences, into big waters in the north, and small waters in the south.

The north Wessex scene is dominated by reservoirs, and none more so than Blagdon. Its 440 acres can realistically be described as the origin of the modern English reservoir fishing, and it still offers excellent sport for the day-ticket bank and boat angler.

Next door neighbour, Chew, offers an even larger venue at 1200 acres. The loss of some of Blagdon's intimacy is compensated for by some of the finest drift fishing in Europe, and it is a major competition venue with stocking and facilities to match. The nearby Barrows complex of 3 smaller reservoirs offers rather less intimidating sport for the bank angler.

To the far west of Somerset, the large reservoirs of Clatworthy, at 130 acres, and Wimbleball, at 374 acres, offer good sport and open, upland scenery, while Hawkridge is more sheltered in a hidden valley near Spaxton.

To the south of the county there are several fisheries of note. Sutton Bingham, near Yeovil, is a clay-based reservoir of 142 acres which offers challenging bank and boat fishing. Viaduct, at Somerton, is a small stillwater which is well stocked and can offer exceptional autumn and winter sport in an area where this is at a premium, and Flowers Farm, just south of Yeovil, offers outstanding scenery and quality fishing, with waters almost as clear as its neighbours to the south on the chalk.

The south Wessex stillwater trout fisheries are almost exclusively small and spring-fed, their chalk waters producing outstanding sport with lots of stalking and sight fishing. Few of the pools on these fisheries exceed a couple of acres, notable exceptions being Steeple Langford to the west of Salisbury at 17 acres, which is one of the very few to offer limited boat fishing, and Avon Springs at Durrington, north of Salisbury, with pools up to 5 acres.

The typical Dorset stillwaters each offer five or six pools, mostly under 2 acres, with stockings predominantly of rainbows from two to ten pounds. Good examples include both Pallington and Wessex Flyfishing near Tolpuddle, and Rockbourne near Fordingbridge.

Though some have dabbled with the monster rainbows stocked in some of their Hampshire counterparts, most have realised that the majority of anglers actually prefer middleweight fish.

Nice Wessex rainbow for Di Cooling.
Picture courtesy Dave Cooling

Book Review

by the Editor

West Country Fly Fishing
An anthology edited by Anne Voss Bark.
ISBN 0-7090-6180-3. £12.99

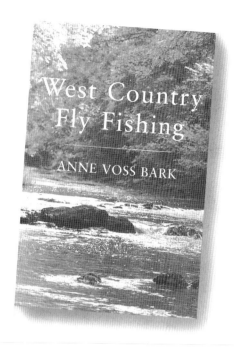

This is not only a book about fly fishing in the west country. It combines some wonderful writing with sound advice on catching the fish and paints a glorious picture of this wonderful part of the country.

Anne Voss Bark owns and runs the Arundell Arms Hotel in Lifton on the Devon - Cornwall border and is well qualified to compile such a book. The Arundell Arms has some 20 miles of beats on the Tamar and tributaries, providing some of the best salmon, sea trout and brown trout fishing in the area.

Contributors include Brian Clarke, angling correspondent of The Times, Ted Hughes, author and Poet Laureate, the late Dermot Wilson, probably the most respected dry fly fisherman in England of his day and 'local boys' Roy Buckingham and David Pilkington (who contributes elsewhere in this guide). The book contains many colour photographs.

Within the pages of this book you can escape to the peace and quiet of streams where you will marvel at the beauty of the surroundings and the fish, small trout by many standards, but truly wild trout. For those anglers who find it hard to understand the appeal of waters where a 12oz trout is large, this book will explain it beautifully.

Salmon fishing is also covered in the book and there is a gem of an article on sea trout fishing by local master Roy Buckingham. Lake fishing is not excluded with mention of waters such as Chew, Blagdon and Stafford Moor.

The book is also interspersed with quotes from various sources dating back to 1853, giving it a timeless feel and making the reader aware that, although methods and equipment may have changed, the essence of the sport is as it ever was.

More and more concern is being expressed from all quarters over the quality of our environment and, specifically, the state of our rivers and streams. Rivers, and the life within them, form a very delicate part of our ecosystem. Damage caused in minutes can take years to repair and many charitable organisations have been established to supplement the work done by the Environment Agency. One such organisation is the Westcountry Rivers Trust, and it is refreshing to note that all royalties from the sale of this book will be given to help them to help us, the anglers.

I'll finish with a quote from the book;

'So give me a light trout rod and the dry fly, and a stream which runs clear through moor or meadow, and I ask no more of the day'

Lord Home, Border Rivers, 1979.

Rod Reviews

by The Editor

Here I go again, the annual 'duffers' rod review, or an honest opinion from someone who probably casts worse than you!. Submissions this year are two rods from Orvis, one from Carbotec and one from Snowbee.

Orvis Clearwater 8'6" 5wt line Full Flex 5.0. RRP £99

This rod is aimed at the 'budget conscious angler' and is the cheapest in the Orvis range. It's still a lot of rod for the money though. It has a reversed half wells grip, uplocking wood and black anodized aluminium reel seat. The finish is excellent, a 'traditional' gloss graphite with dark green whippings, snake rings and a lined butt ring. Supplied in velcro fastening bag and plastic tube.

Orvis Trident TL905 9' 5wt Line Tip Flex 9.5. RRP £410

This is definitely the other end of the market! A deep green finish with whippings to match. A really nice piece of cork for the reversed half wells grip, gold anodized uplocking hardware and a tasty burl maple reel seat. The Trident series are the lightest ever made by Orvis and I can't see how they can be made any lighter! Black titanium Nitride snakes and a lined butt ring complete the fittings. It is supplied in the nicest 'tube' I've ever seen. Covered in burgundy material with an embroidered badge, zip closure, fabric carrying handle and a little 'brass' plaque on the top identifying the model no. It also has an Orvis 25 year unconditional warranty. This means Orvis will repair or replace it, regardless of the cause of damage for 25 years, beat that!

Flex Index. A word about the Orvis Flex Index system of rating rods. For many years rods have been described by adjectives such as tip, middly, stiff, soft etc. So we are well overdue for an industry standard way of describing a rod's action. The Flex Index describes rods on a scale from 2.5 to 12.5, where 2.5-5.5 are full flex (all through), 6.0-

9.0 are mid flex (tip and middle) and 9.5 to 12.5 are tip flex (tip). The Flex Index will enable a rod's action to be accurately described wherever it appears on the scale. A brilliant idea and well overdue! Hopefully all manufacturers will adopt this system.

Carbotec 9' 5wt Line 4 piece. RRP £205

This is the first 4 piece fly rod I have tried. The sections are a mere 28' long so you'll get it in the boot of your mini! Finish is the usual Carbotec deep, translucent amber with whippings to match. Woodgrain uplocking alloy reel seat on a full wells, traditional snakes and lined butt complete the fittings. Supplied in a heavyweight cloth bag and plastic tube. 5 years manufacturers warranty and one year unconditional guarantee, repairing or replacing a damaged rod whatever the cause, is standard throughout the range.

Snowbee Diamond II 9'6" Line wt 6-7. RRP £99.95

A pre-production sample of one of Snowbee's new range. A matt black finish with black whippings, traditional snakes, lined butt ring and black alloy uplocking reel seat on a reversed half wells. I must admit to preferring the matt finish but it wont make any difference to the performance. It is supplied with a bag and final production models of 9' (7-8wt.) and over will have a full wells handle with a butt extension.

IN USE

Clearwater: A real all through action on this, right to the butt. It has a bit of a 'lump' where the two halves join which isn't all that pleasing aesthetically but didn't affect the performance. I didn't expect it to cast that well but I could double haul a whole line out. It also feels delicate on short casting which tends not to happen on stiffer, longer rods.

Trident: Very light, It's described as tip flex but I thought it was a bit middly. Look at the Flex Index though and it's rated 9.5 which is only just tip flex which bears out exactly how it feels. This is a really tasty rod, it feels right, nicely balanced and I'd

Game

13lb December salmon for Chris Marsland.
Butterwell Fishery - River Camel

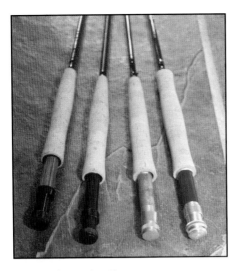

Left to right: Clearwater, Snowbee, Trident, Carbotec.

two (apart from aligning the sections when you put the rod together, How about a little dab of paint or mark to show when sections are properly aligned, on all rods!). This rod really suited me, tip and middle but lots of power and control and happy controlling the line at most lengths.

So that's what I think, four very nice rods, well made, good components. They will all do the job but you do, more or less, get what you pay for. Better quality components, better warranty, nicer presentation. Whether you wish to pay the extra is up to you and your budget but, whichever you decide on **TRY IT FIRST!** Use the reel and line you currently use or get a matched setup at the time and haggle, there are a lot of people trying to sell rods - buyers market! All of the above companies will let you try rods at their premises and they can be found at:

be happy fishing anywhere with it. Power and subtlety personified.

Snowbee: Lots of 'oomph' in this one, shoots a whole line, fairly tippy action but doesn't feel stretched with a long line. Enough flexibility to control a shortish line, plenty of power to control good sized fish.

Carbotec: This certainly doesn't suffer from having 4 sections instead of the usual

ORVIS, 22 Cathedral Yard, Exeter, Devon EX1 1HB. Tel: 01392 272599.

CARBOTEC, Exeter Angling Centre, Adjacent to Fore St., Smythen St., Exeter EX1 1BN. Tel: 01392 436404.

SNOWBEE, Unit 2A Parkway Ind. Est., St. Modwen Rd, Plymouth PL6 8LH. Tel: 01752 672226.

Andrew Whittle from Weston Super Mare with a superbly conditioned rainbow of 12lb 6oz.

Bellbrook Valley

Kevin Melhuish of Exeter with a superb 27lb bag including two brown trout. Stafford Moor

Neil McDermid of Exeter with a 13lb 7oz rainbow on a cats whisker. Bellbrook Valley

Simon Gawesworth has been a regular contributor to Get Hooked since the first issue back in 1994.

Simon and his family have lived in the west country since 1977 where Simon developed his skills and knowledge of fly fishing on the rivers of north Devon.

He features regularly in the finals of national competitions and has fished for England on both rivers and stillwaters.

He has been selected once more to represent England in the 1998 World Championships in Poland.

We would like to thank Simon for his contributions and wish him continued success

Simon Gawesworth 'potholing' for trout on the River L n.
Picture courtesy Russell Symons M.I.P.D.

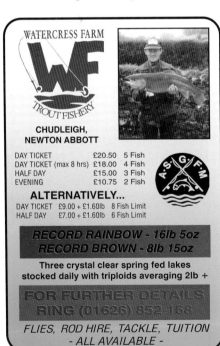

Coarse

Paul Dicks with a 30lb plus mirror from a local syndicate water.
Bristol Angling Centre

The Club Scene

Mike Weaver

Contrary to popular opinion, anglers are sociable creatures, as the number of fishing clubs prove. Many fishermen join their first club to gain access to its waters, and that remains the prime reason for becoming a member of a club or association. However, there are many other motivations, from participating in competitions to sharing a common interest in fly tying.

For the youngster or novice coming into fishing, look out for a club that offers tuition in angling skills; club members have always offered advice to newcomers but often formal courses are available at very low cost.

For as long as anyone can remember, coarse fishing clubs have organised pegged-out competitions, and the skills gained in local events have taken many anglers on to regional, national and even international success. More recently, the growth of reservoir trout fishing has seen a dramatic expansion in loch style competitions, in which anglers fish a team of flies in front of a drifting boat.

The Guild of Fly Dressers, as its name suggests brings together flytyers to hone their skills through sharing knowledge, and local branches organise flytying classes, competitions, lectures and fishing outings.

Many anglers also join the national organisations like the National Federation of Anglers, the Salmon & Trout Association and the National Federation of Sea Anglers, to ensure that fishing has a strong voice in fighting pollution, lobbying Government and protecting the rights of anglers.

Ultimately, however, we come back to the satisfaction of joining a club that owns or leases water for the purpose of maintaining and improving the quality of its fishing and providing fishing for its members. Many anglers soon find that there is far more to fishing than catching fish when they get involved in activities as diverse as bank clearing, fish netting and restocking, gravel digging, stile building, rubbish clearing and generally improving the river or lake environment.

So, if you want to find out what clubs are available to suit your needs, consult a fishing friend, check out the options through your local tackle dealer or turn to the directory starting on page 110 of this guide.

The Salmon & Trout Association
Local contact details

Membership inquiries or requests for advice and information from local Branches of the Salmon and Trout Association are most welcome.

These should be directed to Branch Secretaries, who may be contacted as follows.

Bristol & West
N I Mitchell, 79 Cedrick Road, Bath,
Avon BA1 3PE
Tel: 01179 290611 (home)
01255 424749 (work)

Wessex (incl South Wilts and Dorset)
C A G Wells, Manor Cottage, Shrewton
Wilts SP3 4DB
Tel: 01980 620474

Somerset
J Greene, Breach Barton, West
Bagbrough, Taunton TA4 3EE
Tel: 01823 432006

North Devon
T J C Pearkes, Preston House, Bow,
Crediton, Devon EX17 6EZ
Tel: 01363 82887

South & East Devon & Tamar
E Clarkson, Moss Rose Cottage, Preston,
Kingsteignton, Newton Abbott, S. Devon
Tel: 01626 54284

Cornwall
S Gardiner, 17 Gyllyngvase Terrace
Falmouth, Cornwall TR11 4DL
Tel: 01326 318528

Coarse

Angie Whelan of Barnstaple - 17lb 9oz carp Spires Lakes

PENINSULA COARSE FISHERIES

COARSE FISHING PERMIT AGENTS:

A: The Post Office, Slade, Ilfracombe, Devon, EX34 8LQ
Tel: (01271) 862257
B: Variety Sports, 23 Broad Street,Ilfracombe, Devon.
Tel: (01271) 862039
C: Summerlands Tackle, 3 Golflinks Road, Westward Ho!,
Devon, EX39 1LH. Tel: (01237) 471291
D: The Kingfisher, 22 Castle St,Barnstaple, Devon, EX1 1DR.
Tel: (01271) 344919
E: Powlers Piece Garage, Powlers Piece, East Putford,
Holsworthy, Devon EX22 7XW Tel: (01237) 451282
F: Bude Angling Supplies, 6 Queen Street, Bude, Cornwall.
Tel: (01288) 353396
G: Bideford Tourist Information Centre, The Quay, Bideford,
N. Devon Tel: (01237) 477676
H: Whiskers Pet Centre, 9 High Street, Torrington, Devon.
Tel: (01805) 622859
I: Exeter Angling Centre, Smythen St, Exeter, Devon EX1 1BN
Tel: (01392) 436404
J: Exmouth Tackle & Sports, 20 The Strand,
Exmouth, Devon EX8 1AF. Tel: (01395) 274918
K: Knowle Post Office, Budleigh Salterton. Tel: (01395)
442303
L: Newtown Angling Centre, Newtown, Germoe, Penzance,
Cornwall TR20 9AF. Tel: (01736) 763721
M: Atlantic Fishing Tackle, 36 Wendron Street, Helston,
Cornwall. Tel: (01326) 561640
N: Ironmonger Market Place, St Ives, Cornwall. TR26 1RZ.
Tel: (01736) 796200
O: Heamoor Stores, Heamoor, Gulval, Nr Penzance. TR18
3EJ. Tel: (01736) 65265

LOWER SLADE - Ilfracombe, Devon
Stocked with mirror and common carp to 20lb plus
bream to 5lb plus, perch to 2.25lb, roach, rudd,
gudgeon and pike.
Fishing Times:Open all year, 24 hours per day
Permits: From agents: A,B,C,D. Tel: (01288) 321262

JENNETTS - Bideford, Devon
Best fish: Common 22lb, Mirror 23lb. Produces quality
bags of smaller carp, roach, and tench to float & pole.
Fishing Times: Open all year, 6.30am to 10pm.
Permits: From agents: C,F,G, Tel: (01288) 321262

DARRACOTT - Torrington, Devon
Roach up to 1lb. Mixed bags to 20lb plus of roach,
rudd, bream, tench, perch to 2.25lb, carp to 15lb.
Fishing Times: Open all year, 24 hours per day.
Permits: From agents: C,D,F,G,H,
Seasons Permits - Peninsula Fisheries (01837) 871565
Tel: (01288) 321262

MELBURY - Bideford, Devon
Best mirror 27.75lb. Good mixed bags of roach, rudd,
bream to pole, float and feeder.
Fishing Times: Open all year. 6.30am - 10pm.
Permits: From agents: C,D,E,F,G
Limited season permits from our office.
Tel: (01288) 321262

TRENCHFORD - Nr Christow, Devon
Pike weighing up to 30lbs.
Fishing Times: 1 October to 31 March inclusive.
1 hour before sunrise to 1 hour after sunset.
Permits: Self service kiosk at Kennick Reservoir

UPPER TAMAR LAKE - Bude, Cornwall
Carp to 28lbs. 50lb plus bags of bream and 30lb bags
of rudd. Regular competitions.
Fishing Times: Open all year, 24 hours a day.
Permits: From agents: C,D,F Tel: (01288) 321262

SQUABMOOR - Exmouth, Devon
Good head of carp to 25lb, roach to 3lb 2oz, Tench.
Fishing Times Open all year, 24 hours a day.
Permits: From agents: I,J,K
Season Permits from our office Tel: 01837 871565

OLD MILL - Dartmouth, Devon
Carp to over 20lbs, roach to 2lb, tench and bream.
Fishing Times: Open all year, 24 hours a day.
Permits: Season permits from our Office
Tel: (01837) 871565

PORTH - Newquay, Cornwall
Bags of 130lb plus have been caught. Best bream 9lb
2oz, tench 9lb 12oz. rudd to 3lb, roach to 1.25lb plus.
Mixed bags of roach, rudd/skimmers to 60lb.
Fishing Times: Open all year, 24 hours a day
Permits: Agents L,M. Self service at Porth car park.
Season permits from our Office. Great competition
water. Tel: (01637) 877959

BOSCATHNOE - Penzance, Cornwall
Common, mirror and crucian carp with fish into the
low 20lb range. Roach and bream also stocked.
Fishing Times: Open all year, 1 hour before sunrise to 1
hour after sunset. Season permits from our Office.
Permits: From agents: L,M,N,O. Tel: (01579) 342366

COLLEGE - Nr Falmouth, Cornwall
Carp to 20lb plus. Best fish: carp 26lb, bream 8lb 6oz,
tench 8lb 8oz and eel 7lb, Pike over 30lb.
Fishing Times: Open all year, 24 hours per day.
Permits: From agents: L,M and self service unit at
Argal Reservoir car park.
Season permits from our Office (01837) 871565.
Tel (01579) 342366

BUSSOW - St Ives, Cornwall
Rudd to 1.5lb, roach bream and carp.
Fishing Times: Open all year, 24 hours a day.
Permits: From agents: L,N. Season permits from our
Office. Tel (01579) 342366

CRAFTHOLE - Nr. Torpoint, Devon.
Stocked with carp and tench.
Quality Carp up to 30lb.
Fishing Times: Open all year
1hr before sunrise to 1hr
after sunset.
Limited season permits
from our office (01837)
871565

Coarse

Craig King with 5lb 12oz tench from Tockenham Lake, Lyneham.
Bristol Bath & Wiltshire A.A.

—The—
Royalty
Fishery

"The sight of golden flanks over gravel rarely fails to produce a reaction." Such is the lure of the Royalty that both John Wilson and Andy Little have made films here.

Of course for anyone who's heard of the Royalty, they will know that it's best known for its barbel fishing. Anglers travel from all over the country to fish for barbel here. The fish grow particularly fast on this water and during October last year the anglers were catching two or three doubles a week. During summer when the water is clear, it is possible to search out the fish with a good pair of Polaroid's and some roving tackle.

When I was approached to write this piece, I happily said yes at the chance to promote the Fishery and tell the general public what's going on. The problem is where to start. The Royalty has a fantastic range of fishing, varying from quality game fishing to specimen carp fishing. Nor is this fishing spread over a number of different waters. It is all based on one of Britain's finest chalk rivers, the Hampshire Avon. The Fishery is situated at the lower end and covers the area from just above Christchurch, down through the town and into the harbour.

Coarse Fishing

Recent years have seen the appearance of more and more carp on the river. Last year the first one over 30 lbs was caught. If you think that these fish don't compare with the 40's and 50's caught on lakes then think again. These fish

were born and grew up on the fast flowing Avon water, and as such are found and can be caught all over the Fishery. Come with strong line if you want to take them on.

During the winter the pike angler is king. The pike season on the Royalty opens on 1 November and runs through to the close season. I have been on the water for three years and have lost count of the number of twenties caught in both years.

The joys of Game Fishing on the Royalty

If you are more interested in game fishing or would like to start then this is a good place to come. We have regular salmon rods which fish from 15 March - 20 June. Outside these dates day rods can be obtained and there's always a good chance of connecting with a lively grilse in July or August. We take advance bookings on several pools which provide a variety of game and coarse fishing. Amongst these, the Bridge Pool ranks as one of the best sea trout pools in Southern England.

This is situated right in the middle of Christchurch next to the Priory providing an idyllic setting.

What's new at the Royalty?

This year should see the return of the Parlour Pool. Renowned for salmon and barbel fishing, it has been out of action for

A 12lb 12oz barbel from the Royalty for Mark Bonham

Coarse

16lb 8oz common caught by Mr Hart.
Abbey Lakes (specimen lakes).

the last year due to operational work. In November last year we released another 1,000 one year old barbel. The fish released last year were all marked with a blue dot on their belly. This was done so that anglers would know if they catch any and be able to tell us. (If you come down please join in this scheme.

It's also hoped that by June this year we will have a new wider footbridge across the river. This should allow greater access for disabled anglers to fish in more locations. This is part of our ongoing drive to help all parts of the local community enjoy the fishing.

Helping You Out

If the above information seems a bit overawing at first sight, then why not come down and find out more. We have two full time bailiffs who are always more than happy to help. They can often put you in the best spot or tell you the best tactics to use. Besides the Bailiffs, the Royalty has two car parks for convenience, both situated very close to the water (If you let the handbrake off in the Lower car park you may find yourself a bit closer to the water than you wished!). We take great pride in the way we look after the river and the bankside. We also have two sets of toilets on site for those who find themselves caught out (no pun intended of course).

All these features mean that the Royalty is not only a good place to come and avidly hunt out specimen fish, its also a good place to come and relax. Prices on the Fishery start at £5 for concessionary tickets and rise to £8 for a day permit. Those entitled to a concessionary ticket include OAP's juveniles and disabled anglers. If you would like to know more please feel free to contact me on the number below or ring the bailiffs on their number. I look forward to seeing you on the river.

Matthew Stammers, Fisheries Manager
01202 591111 ext. 3331
Bailiffs - 01202 485262
mobile 0802 761417

Two succesful and happy anglers, depite the weather!

West Pitt

Coarse

Peter Ferguson with a 13lb 8oz 'ghostie'.
Milemead

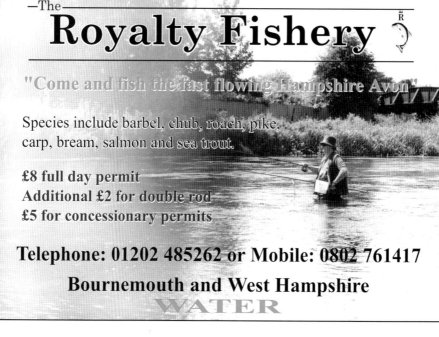

Westcountry Rivers Trust

Making a difference

The Westcountry Rivers Trust was established in 1995 to protect and enhance the region's rivers, streams and wetlands for the benefit of farmers, fishermen and the wider community. The Trust aims to achieve its objectives through practical improvements, through advice and support to the individuals and organisations that own and manage these waters and through the education of all sectors of the community on the issues that influence these shared resources.

The Westcountry Rivers Trust really came of age during 1997, growing in stature and gaining respect, initiating and running a wide range of projects. The Tamar 2000 Project in particular enabled the Rivers Trust to show that it can successfully design, fund, administer and deliver a new integrated approach to river rehabilitation, tackling not only the symptoms but also the causes of the river's decline. This groundbreaking work on a catchment scale is now capturing the attention of those at the highest level of government and its agencies. Importantly on the ground, not only is this approach continually bringing about physical improvements to the river environment, it is engaging the farming community and others in achieving them.

Over the year the Rivers Trust has been fortunate to host a number of field visits from VIPs including, Lord Donoughue (MAFF), Lord De Ramsey (Environment Agency) and Lord Rothschild (Heritage Lottery Fund). Each has been impressed by The Trust's work and in every case The Trust has had very favourable feedback with a strong indication of support.

The Rivers Trust has identified a number

Coarse

*A beautifully conditioned 20lb common for A. Groves of Exeter.
Simpson Valley*

of important areas and has drawn up proposals for three partnership projects with the Environment Agency with applications pending for funding. The first of these is a project on the Torridge to rehabilitate the Waldon tributary.

Through its work the Trust is delivering a number of environmental and conservation targets identified in National and Regional Biodiversity Action Plans including those in the Atlantic Salmon Biodiversity Action Plan.

The Trust has already been hugely successful in raising the awareness of freshwater issues and attracting funding to this area. It has developed new broad approaches designed from the bottom up to appeal to a wide section of the community and to all political shades. It is earning the respect of other organisations and is now very well placed to play a major partnership role in the management and rehabilitation of our freshwater heritage.

To improve their chances of raising money from grant sources to help coarse and game angling in the region The Trust needs to be able to demonstrate the financial commitment and goodwill of the fishermen of the South West.

The Trust asks every fisherman, fishing club, fishery owner, tackle shop, fishing hotel, pub or guest house to send them a donation so that they can clean up your rivers streams and ponds. If you can afford to, The Trust asks individuals to covenant £50 a year (less that £1 per week) towards the work of the Trust and ask groups, clubs, businesses and organisations to covenant £100 per year to help the Trust achieve these improvements. In return The Trust will circulate magazines and invitations to events and activities and allow clubs, groups, shops and other organisations to use their logo in advertising and publications - showing that you care enough to help Westcountry fishermen and the waters that they cherish.

For further information contact Arlin Rickard, The Director, Westcountry Rivers Trust, Bradford Lodge, Blisland, Bodmin, Cornwall PL30 4LF.

VRANCH HOUSE SCHOOL FLY FISHING CHARITY CHALLENGE 1998

In aid of the Devon & Exeter Spastics Society

Pairs of anglers are invited to enter the 7th Fly Fishing Charity Challenge to raise funds for children with cerebral palsy at Vranch House School & Centre, Exeter. The Challenge, originally sponsored by Airflo, has raised a magnificent £45,500 since 1992.

Heats will take place from April to September at Innis, Tree Meadow, St Merryn, Rose Park, Temple, Roadford, Kennick, Stafford Moor, Watercress, Tavistock and Bellbrook Valley. There are over £3,000 worth of prizes including M & S vouchers, lines, day tickets, garden statues and hooks. Entry is free provided the minimum sponsorship of £20 per person is raised. For details please contact the fisheries or Sue Gould, Marketing Manager of the Devon & Exeter Spastics Society: Tel Exeter 01392 873543.

Heat Dates:

Bellbrook Valley	Tiverton	01398 351292	Sun 5th April
Kennick Reservoir	Bovey Tracey	01626 865739	Sun 3rd May
Innis Fishery	St Austell	01726 851162	Sun 10th May
St Merryn	Padstow	01841 533090	Sun 17th May
Temple	Bodmin	01208 850250	Sun 31st May
Tree Meadow	Hayle	01736 850899	Sun 19th July
Watercress	Chudleigh	01626 852168	Sun 2nd Aug
Tavistock	Tavistock	01822 615441	Sun 23rd Aug
Stafford Moor	Winkleigh	01805 804360	Sun 30th Aug
Rose Park	Launceston	01566 86278	TBA
Roadford Lake	Okehampton	01837 87534	TBA

Coarse

Jeff Parker Junior with a quality bream.
Bristol Bath & Wiltshire A.A.

The Angling Trade Association

The maxim 'a business which loses its customers is doomed' applies equally to many other facets of life, including sport. Most national angling bodies do not have the organisation or financial resources to mount effective campaigns to promote the sport, which makes the Angling Trade Association's (ATA) continuing initiatives so important.

For more than 25 years, the Association and its sister body - the Angling Foundation have been supported by most major tackle manufacturers in promoting angling to newcomers. The various schemes have been highly effective, and the success of 1997 should herald a boost for angling in the forthcoming 12 months.

'Give Angling a Go'

In acknowledgement that the best way to introduce people to angling is to teach them at the water's edge, the ATA initiated the 'Give Angling a Go' scheme in summer 1996. The scheme - which targets organised groups of new and would-be anglers - operates in conjunction with most other major bodies, including the National Federation of Anglers, The Salmon and Trout Association, the National Federation of Sea Anglers, the Commercial Coarse Fisheries Association, the Association of Professional Game Fishery Managers and the Environment Agency.

Its aim is to bring more people to the sport by giving them advice, guidance and a taste of fishing under the supervision of experienced anglers. Originally aimed at teenagers and slightly younger children, those running the scheme are equally happy to assist any group interested in trying the sport for the first time.

During the last year the 'Give Angling a Go' scheme has been successful in arranging for numerous groups of young people to enjoy a days fishing. These trips

have taken place at various Commercial Coarse Fisheries throughout the country under the watchful eyes of coaches drawn from teams sponsored by the ATA's member companies.

Mission Impossible

The largest event to date occurred at a fishery complex in West Sussex where one enthusiastic youth worker came up with her own version of 'Mission Impossible' by asking if 120 children - aged 9 to 15 - could go fishing on the same day at the same venue! In fact, when she had offered the youngsters a wide choice of sports, they opted for angling.... a testament to how attitudes to the sport are changing for the better.

The day was a huge success, thanks in no small way to an army of willing helpers drawn from the ranks of many of the bodies supporting the 'Give Angling a Go' scheme. The angling press played a valuable part too, by helping with the coaching and ensuring that the day was well covered in angling newspapers and periodicals The

continued on page 68

Tommy Pickering with young Telegraph winner

Fish on at Westpitt

Coarse

Jerry Nugent with a good size pike. Retallack.

publicity even included cable television coverage throughout Sussex.

An equally daunting challenge arose in mid-summer when 30 young people asked to try sea fishing for a day. The children were able to enjoy a fantastic day's fishing from the shore and from chartered boats under the supervision of various sea-fishing internationals. The key to the success of the event was the active participation of the National Federation of Sea Anglers and the National Federation of Chartered Skippers.

Not just for the Boys

To help publicise the joys of trout fishing, the 'Give Angling a Go' scheme staged a special day for lady journalists. Having tried fishing, they were invited to cook what they had caught under expert guidance from a top chef. Before the day began, the women shared the widely held feelings of uncertainty about capturing, handling and cleaning fish. By the end of the day they had been converted, and they all expressed the wish to try angling again.

The scheme also gave one young angler the day of a lifetime. The golden opportunity arose following a competition featured in the 'Young Telegraph', the youth supplement of the Daily Telegraph. The lucky winner was selected from thousands of entries, and he won the right to fish with former World Champion Tommy Pickering.

Any organised group of no more than 5 young people with its own transport can apply to 'Give Angling a Go' by writing to the Regency Business Centre, Queens Road, Kenilworth Warwickshire, CV8 1JQ.

New ideas for 1998 include a national 'Give Angling a Go' day to be arranged in April with the support of the major angling organisations. Details are still being finalised, but they will include 'two for the price of one' ticket offers at Commercial Coarse Fisheries and free fishing at selected trout fisheries throughout Britain

'Take a Friend Fishing'

It is a feature of angling that most people are introduced to the sport by a family member or friend. With this in mind, the Angling Foundation has been running its 'Take a Friend Fishing' campaign for more than a decade. Although it has taken many guises, it now centres on the provision of free information packs aimed at four target groups - new anglers, returning anglers, individuals who wish to take other people fishing and the organisers of group 'try it' sessions. They include information sheets, a colour newspaper, special stickers and guide leaflets.

The packs are free and can be ordered in any multiple from 1-500 by writing to the Regency Business Centre address given earlier.

National Fishing Week

The Angling Trade Association also plays an important role in promoting UK National Fishing Week, held each year during the last week in August. In 1997 some 250,000 participated in a range of events throughout the country backed by free rod licences offered by the Environment Agency.

Such has been the success of the initiative since its inception in 1992 that there has been a year-on-year increase in the number of people taking part. The organisers are confident that at some future stage, they will be able to boast that they have brought more than a million people to the bank during the week, making it THE key event in the annual angling calendar.

Anyone interested in taking part in UK National Fishing Week, as either an organiser or as a participant, can obtain more details from National Fishing Week Headquarters, 23 Southdown Road, Thatcham, Berkshire, RGT9 3BF.

Centres of Excellence

Among other ideas, which will come to fruition in the next 12 months, is a scheme to establish a network of 'centres of angling excellence'. Each centre will be granted an award if it is able to provide young people with all they need to receive angling tuition under expert guidance.

Through these and other initiatives, the Angling Trade Association can be proud of its enviable record of success in promoting the sport to new generations. With such careful but substantial investment, angling is well placed to face the future with confidence.

Coarse

Two fine chub of 4lb plus and 2lb plus caught at Freshford by Mike Staite. Bristol Bath & Wilts A.A.

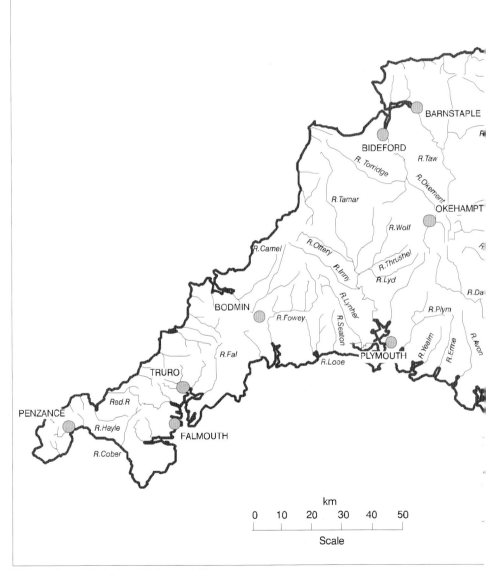

BARNSTAPLE

BIDEFORD

R.Taw

R. Torridge

R.Okement

R.Tamar

OKEHAMPT

R.Wolf

R.Camel

R.Ottery

R.Inny

R.Thrushel

R.Lyd

R.Lynher

R.Da

R.Plym

BODMIN

R.Fowey

R.Seaton

PLYMOUTH

R.Yealm

R.Erme

R.Avon

R.Fal

R.Looe

TRURO

Red.R

PENZANCE

R.Hayle

FALMOUTH

R.Cober

km

| 0 | 10 | 20 | 30 | 40 | 50 |

Scale

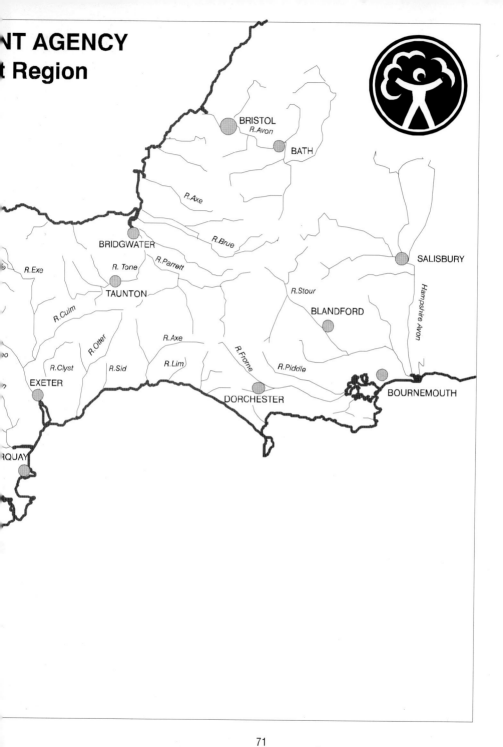

NT AGENCY
t Region

BRISTOL
R.Avon

BATH

R.Axe

R.Brue

BRIDGWATER

R.Exe

R. Tone

R.Parrett

SALISBURY

TAUNTON

R.Stour

BLANDFORD

Hampshire Avon

R.Culm

R.Axe

R.Otter

R.Frome

R.Piddle

R.Clyst

R.Sid

R.Lim

EXETER

DORCHESTER

BOURNEMOUTH

RQUAY

Coarse Fishing in the South Wessex area

by Matt Carter

The South Wessex area has a reputation for consistently offering coarse fishing of exceptional quality. Historically the area has produced many record breaking fish including C F Warrick's pike of 37lbs in the 1940s, Aylmer Tryon's record 'Avon' barbel of 14lb 6oz from the same period, and, more recently a roach record of 4lbs 3oz set by R.N. Clarke in 1990 from the Dorset Stour. Annually specimen fish of near record breaking proportions are reported in captures from this area.

The principal rivers that offer coarse fishing in the South Wessex Area include the famous 'Hampshire' Avon, Dorset Stour and Frome. Notable limits of coarse fishing on the River Avon extend from Salisbury, downstream approximately 60km to Christchurch. Coarse fishing on the River Stour extends from Gillingham, near its source, downstream some 60km to Christchurch where it forms a common estuary with the River Avon before meeting the sea.

Limited sections of the River Frome are open to coarse fishing, mainly near Dorchester and Wareham. Other coarse fisheries in South Wessex include a short section of the Kennet and Avon Canal and numerous ponds, lakes and gravel pits.

Fishing rights are generally controlled by local angling clubs and the appropriate permit must be obtained before fishing. It is important to note that a valid Environment Agency Rod Licence is also required when fishing any of these waters; licences can be obtained from all post offices as well as from the local Environment Agency office.

Roach can be caught throughout the area from the aforementioned rivers, as well as from many lakes. Larger specimens of 2lbs and over can be located on most stretches of the River Avon and in more isolated areas of the Rivers Stour and Frome. In particular good sized fish are commonly reported from the middle Avon at Fordingbridge downstream to Ibsley, whilst the Wimborne area on the River Stour has a reputation for producing big roach. Specimen roach are often caught in the lower reaches of the River Frome at Wareham. Larger catches of smaller fish can be made in the tidal section of the River Stour at Iford. Radipole Lake in Weymouth can offer some good quality roach fishing during the winter months.

Chub can be found throughout the Rivers Avon and Stour, but are absent from the River Frome. Large specimens of up to 7lbs are caught annually from the middle and lower reaches of the River Avon. Whilst specimens of these proportions are infrequent on the River Stour, reports of chub of up to 6lbs are not uncommon. Favoured sections on the River Avon include Burgate, East Mills, Bickton, Ibsley, Winkton and the famous Royalty Fishery in Christchurch. Large chub can be found on the River Stour from Wimborne downstream to the famous Throop fishery near Christchurch.

Barbel are common throughout the River Avon and present in the middle and lower reaches of the River Stour. Specimens of up to 14lbs are reported each year from the middle and lower Avon. Fish over 10lbs are often recorded at the Throop fishery on the River Stour. Bream can now be found throughout the Rivers Avon and Stour, as well as in a number of local gravel pits. Large catches of bream on the Avon have been made from the Royalty Fishery in Christchurch with individual specimens of up to 8lbs in weight being caught.

Good catches of bream can also be made on the River Stour near Sturminster Newton, Blandford and downstream at Iford. Bream can be fished for at Peters Finger Lake near Salisbury. Dace seem to be making a come back in the area and good sport can be expected from many stretches

Coarse

Three excellent perch, all over 2lb, caught from the top lake. Stowford Grange.

of the Avon, Stour and Frome. In particular good numbers of dace can be found in the sections of river near Salisbury, Ringwood, Iford, Wimborne, Blandford and Wareham.

Carp can now be found throughout most of the rivers in the South Wessex Area. Fish of over 30lbs have been caught on the lower Avon and specimens near 30lbs recorded on the lower Stour. More commonly carp fishing takes place in local lakes and gravel pits.

There are many still waters in the area containing carp and those found near Ringwood provide notable sport with the opportunity of catching fish up to 40lbs. Other still waters selected from a long list include Radipole Lake in Weymouth, Pallington Lakes and Warmwell Lake near Dorchester.

Good tench fishing can also be found in still waters in the Ringwood area, as well as Steeple Langford near Salisbury, and Pallington Lakes near Dorchester. Rudd can be found in many still waters in the area although few hold notable specimens; one such water can be found in the Hyde Lake complex near Wareham.

Large pike can be caught throughout the area from the aforementioned rivers and numerous still waters. It is advised that all pike should be returned to the water unharmed in the same way as other coarse fish. Perch can also be caught throughout the area in rivers and many still waters.

It is important to note that anglers share the river bank and pondside with many other people, animals and plants, therefore it is important to enjoy and respect this environment. This can be achieved by taking litter and waste fishing tackle home to be disposed of properly, and to carefully return all coarse fish back to the water after capture. It is advised to consider the use of barbless hooks and to minimise the use of keepnets.

Coarse

Keith Elmer with a 3lb 6oz bream caught on double red maggot in February. Elmfield

Coarse

21lb 12oz mirror for Simon Stevens.
Island Lake at Salmon Hutch

From Little Fishes

By Douglas Hulme

I have spent all of my professional life, 26 years to date, trying to teach youngsters with special needs. Sometimes it has been relatively simple things such as mathematical addition or how to write a sentence that someone else might understand. At other times it has been things much more mystical, such as why we don't (usually) steal from each other, why it is good to help someone else, why it is (generally) a good idea not to use physical violence and other such aspects of our spiritual being!

Never in all those years however have I ever managed to impart such knowledge as a child learns whilst fishing. Knowledge which passes mere facts and abilities and borders on the realms of something much greater. Let me explain by introducing you to some of the children who have passed through our charity Second Chance.

John suffered from a growth disease, it prevented him from growing at the speed he should have done, which left him at nearly fifteen years of age with a height and stature of a ten or eleven year old boy. He attended a special school for children with moderate learning difficulties, not surprising for someone who lacked confidence and always sought the easy option of not trying rather than trying and failing. His peers in the neighbourhood would make him the butt of their humour with taunts such as John attending a school for "nutters" and the use of boxes to gain stature for such activities as kissing girls.

John was invited for a day's carp fishing in north London, courtesy of second chance. The day went well, there was good support including members of the angling Press. John caught a double figure carp, his first fish ever, landed in front of an appreciative audience of fellow anglers both old and young. The audience grew larger with the publication of colour photographs in weekly newspapers and angling magazines. A star was born. Those neighbourhood peers could be heard seeking advice as to the best methods for catching such a leviathan fish, adults expressed appreciation of the feat and admired the photographs. A change came over John, a new hairstyle, a spring to his step, a willingness to take part in classroom activities, a nonchalant attitude to being wrong in the belief that you could get it right next time. What a lesson one fish had taught this young man, what a transformation.

We all thrive on success but how do you teach success? I would suggest that unless you are a fish you cannot teach it, all you can do is try to create it, but I have witnessed the lesson of success as taught by a fish.

Lessons in life are rarely easily gained and can often be painful, but lessons from the fish can be both on the theme of life itself and enjoyable, even exhilarating, as well.

Second Chance is a serious social working agency in it's own right. There is nothing unusual about this and there is a myriad of other charities and statutory bodies that can claim the same status, but what makes Second Chance so unique is the role that angling and anglers play in the way it works with young people as old as twenty one. Is it sheer coincidence that the charity has a success rate the envy of all in its field? I think not. I am sure it has something to do with one of the greatest educators of all, the fish!

The above is an extract from the anthology "Lessons from the fish", published by Swan Hill Press and available through all booksellers by quoting - ISBN 1 85310 8189

The charity can be contacted at:

Second Chance House,
Somers Road Bridge,
Portsmouth,
Hants PO5 4NS

Tel/Fax 01705 872790

Coarse

Ian Guyatt with a 12lb carp off the top. Witherington Farm

Barbel of 12lb 12oz, 10lb and 7lb 8oz caught by Peter Garbutt on the Bristol Avon. Bristol, Bath & Wiltshire A.A.

Coarse

Beautiful 21lb 3oz mirror for
Keith Bowden.
Creedy

Coarse

A perfect common of 14lb 7oz.
Bush Farm

Coarse

Quality 2lb 2½oz roach for Don Stidwell.
Milemead

Sharpen your Image

Brochures
Stationery
Corporate Identity
General Advertising

Britain's Anglers land more Gold Medals than any other sport

By Rodney Coldron
Press & Media Manager
NATIONAL FEDERATION OF ANGLERS

WHY IS angling such a turn on for Britain's massive army of four million participants?

More people go fishing (8.2% of the population) than play or watch football and it is easily the biggest participant sport In the UK. In Western Europe 30 million people go fishing regularly (Millwood Brown) and, if the gradual increase in teams participating in the World Championships is anything to go by, more and more people are becoming hooked on the sport.

To the uninitiated coarse fishing Is a worm at one end and a fool at the other but a dedicated angler can convince anyone in seconds that fishing is a sport requiring a substantial amount of skill and a tiny slice of good luck! Any angler will explain that fishing is a battle of wits and an exercise in displaying more patience than the human body was designed to have!

Fishing is a sport with no barriers. There is no limit on age, sex, physical ability, education or finance. The young, old, rich, poor, fit and those with disabilities all enjoy the sport.
One of the most famous anglers of all time was Izaak Walton who wrote the 'Compleat Angler' in 1653. He would hardly have expected his book to become the second biggest selling book next to the Bible but his publication had a dramatic influence on the sport in the UK. Perhaps Bernard Venables 'Mr Crabtree Goes Fishing' is the best loved fishing book of all time. Superbly Illustrated and written by Venables in the

Coarse

Carp and bream caught on the Avon at Keynsham.
Bristol, Bath & Wilts A.A.

mid 50's this fantastic book sent people running down to the bankside in their thousands and arguably set more youngsters on the route to coarse fishing than any other publication.

Bernard Venables painted a scene which explained it all. The cautious chub lying beneath an overhanging tree, the superb crimson and gold colouring of a rudd, the enormous power of the barbel, the huge spatula shaped fins and the tiny red eye of the muscular tench, the fear and admiration of the sharp toothed pike and the multi-coloured sparkle of the roach ... the anglers favourite fish.

To some people the fascination of a day in the countryside is reward enough and catching a fish is of secondary importance! The chance to see a kingfisher working, a dragonfly flitting along the bankside or a grass snake swimming across the river may well be regarded as a privilege to the less serious angler, while the real angling enthusiast would want to count or weigh his catch at the end of the day and talk forever more of the one that got away!

Competition fishing is far more serious, with the trophies usually claimed by the experts. England has a formidable record In the World Championships and manager Dick Clegg's Drennan Team England is the most feared angling team in the land. In Hungary last year England's Alan Scotthorne from Barnsley retained his world crown and the team finished runners-up. Dick Clegg MBE also proved our ladies are a force to be reckoned with and Wendy Locker from Chester collected gold while Doncaster's Sandra Halkon•Hunt was runner-up. The Angling Plus England ladies team proved to be outstanding, finishing on top of the world in Portugal in 1997

The National Federation of Anglers is the governing body for coarse fishing in this country. The NFA represents 250,000 members and has around 500 affiliated clubs spread throughout eight regions. The NFA was formed in 1903 to look after the interests of the sport by protecting the aquatic environment from pollution, water abstraction, land drainage schemes and promoting Research and Development into the sport. The aims and objectives established in those early days are still a fundamental part of the Federation's thinking. The NFA has its own headquarters at Egginton Junction in Derbyshire and President Ken Ball says "There can be no better sport to be involved in than angling. Anglers are the 'eyes and ears' of the countryside and we know instantly when something is wrong. We stock the waters and ensure the environment is right for the fish. No one cares more than anglers about the state of our waters.

Angling can claim to be the most successful sport in the UK during 1997. While athletics could only boast of one gold medal in 1997. England's anglers brought home three gold medals, three silvers and two bronze. "This is an achievement the country should be proud of" says England Manager Dick Clegg.

Can there be anything to beat the excitement of seeing the float dip for the first time? The thrill of landing the very first fish? The disbelief in losing a 'monster' fish which shed the hook at the net?

If you haven't tried angling then you must. Ask your local tackle shop for some advice and join a local club. Become an individual member of the NFA for £5 per year and prepare for a June 16 start to the season or find out where there is a pond or lake which offers fishing all the year round. Don't forget you must purchase a weekly or yearly Environment Agency licence before you cast a line anywhere.

Give angling a go. Get down to the waterside and find out what makes us all tick!

TIGHT LINES!!

For more information contact the National Federation of Anglers, Halliday House, Egginton Junction, Derbyshire, DE65 6GU Telephone (01283) 734735

Coarse

Ian Heaps - winner of the competition on this day.
Bush Farm

Luck and Stuff

By the Editor

Even the most professional and experienced of anglers must admit to there being a large degree of luck involved in the sport.

Perhaps luck isn't the right word, it's more 'unpredictability'. I'm sure most have caught a species or size of fish which was completely unexpected at the time. This has to be one of the attractions of the sport. The anticipation when watching the float dip, hearing the buzzer blip, feeling the fly line tighten, whatever the method of detection you can never be sure what's on the other end.

An occasion springs to mind last February when I took Josh and Alf (two sons aged 11 and 9) to local coarse water Elmfield Fisheries. Just going in February was unexpected to start with. It's normally very cold but we were having a spell of unusually mild weather and it was a bit of a spur of the moment thing.

The boys both fished with whips and pole rigs (saves me a lot of time undoing tangles) and I used a 11ft match rod and waggler set up. For the fist 3 hours they out fished me completely. Maggot was the bait and they were catching small roach, rudd and perch. The wind changed direction at about 10am and we moved to new swims to keep the wind behind us. The boys continued to land fish with a couple of bream now amongst the catch. I'd been helping the boys, showing them how to unhook the fish and use a disgorger but decided it was time to sit down and fish properly for an hour.

I just loose fed with maggots, little and often, and caught a perch of about 10oz followed by a bream of a pound or so but the next time the float dipped I struck and nothing moved. Then line started to run off the reel as something large started off across the lake. I was using 4lb line straight through so knew I stood a good chance of landing the fish as long as the hook held and I had the patience to tire the fish on an underpowered rod. The other problem was the pathetic landing net I'd brought. I have

perfectly good landing nets, large and small but couldn't find them this morning and the only one I could find had a 5ft handle and a head about 1ft across.

The boys were pretty excited and we hadn't even seen the fish as it swam up and down in front of us, hugging the bottom. Inevitably the fish did begin to tire and broke surface for the first time. There was a chorus of 'Wow!' from behind me as we got our first glimpse of a carp and a double at that. The owner of the fishery happened to turn up at this moment and did a great job of getting the fish in the net. A beautiful common estimated at 14lb (no scales to weigh it!) was quickly photographed and returned.

A classic case of me being lucky? Certainly was, it took a degree of experience to play and land the fish but, as Alfie proved later by losing a good fish on the whip when the hook pulled out, the fish could have just as easily have picked up someone else's bait. This style of fishing must be the most commonly practised, loose feeding with bits of hookbait, fishing with a float and catching whatever comes along. Really enjoyable, especially when you get 'lucky'.

Luck or skill? Alfie reckons it's skill!

Coarse

19lb 2oz mirror carp.
Spires Lakes

Coarse

Clive with his first double?
Middle Boswin

Supplies & Services

An Emerald Pool double

89

Supplies & Services/Tackle

*7lb Sea Trout from the Teign at Dunsford
caught by Andy Coyne from Axminster.
Robert Jones Fly Fishing*

90

Supplies & Services/Tackle

Specimen bream of 7lb.
Stowford Grange (bottom lake)

Stuart Fivash with possibly the biggest golden tench in the U.K. at 7lb 2oz.
Anglers Paradise

Tackle

12lb mirror carp from Upham Farm. Opposite: Paul Dicks with a 22lb pike from Cheddar Reservoir.

Tackle

Two young anglers very pleased with this 14lb common.
Legge

Where to Stay

Where to Stay

Nice Carp.
Westpitt

Where to Stay

Do you think he's pleased?
Boscastle Peganina

Where to Stay

Joelene Lunn with a Bream from the Crane stretch of the Bristol Avon.
Veals

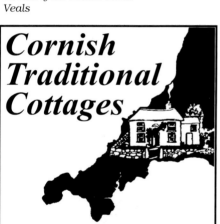

Where to Stay

Rick Perry from Boyton, near Launceston with a 8lb 8oz Golden Rainbow.
Stafford Moor

103

CUT OUT POLLUTION NOW!

Telephone this number anywhere in England and Wales to report:

- **Damage or danger to the natural environment**
- **Pollution**
- **Poaching**
- **Risks to wildlife**
- **Fish in distress**
- **Illegal dumping of hazardous waste**
- **Flooding incidents (for reporting flooding only)**

EMERGENCY HOTLINE

CALL FREE, 24 HRS A DAY, 7 DAYS A WEEK

ENVIRONMENT AGENCY
EMERGENCY HOTLINE

0800 807060

CALL FREE, 24 HRS A DAY, 7 DAYS A WEEK

ENVIRONMENT AGENCY

Help us to protect the environment.

Cut out this card and keep it close to your telephone

DON'T IGNORE IT!
REPORT IT!

ENVIRONMENT AGENCY

SEA FISHING ASSOCIATIONS

National Federation Of Sea Anglers
Head Office: 51A Queen Street, Newton Abbot, Devon. TQ12 2QJ.
Tel/Fax 01626 331330

S.W. Federation Of Sea Anglers
Sec: Stan Rowe. 46 The Roundway, Kingkerswell, Newton Abbot,
Devon. TQ12 5BW

Bristol Channel Federation of Sea Anglers
Keith Reed, 27 St Michaels Avenue, Clevedon, N. Somerset.
Tel: 01275 872101

Cornish Federation of Sea Anglers
Mrs Camilla Perry, 7 Henwood Crescent, St Columb Minor, Newquay,
Cornwall TR7 3HG

Sea Fishing in Cornwall

Atlantic Inn
Contact: Roger Baker. Peverell Terrace, Porthleven, Helston, Cornwall.
TR13 9DZ 01326 562439
Water: Surf - fishing South Cornwall Coast.
Species: Bass (Dicentrarchus labrax).
Permits: Pro - Bass fishing guide.
Charges: £20pp incl tackle 3 - 4hr session from shore. £35pp from
boat 7hrs (Max 4 persons).
Season: May till November.
Methods: Fly fishing, Lure fishing, Bait - fishing.

Boscastle Peganina
Contact: Ken Cave. Tel: 01288 353565

Cornish Sea Angling
Contact: Tom Arnull. Tel: 01736 756162
Water: Rock and Beach Angling from Cornish Coast.

Fish Cornwall
Contact: Terry or Gerry. Gwel-An-Mor Guesthouse, Trevarrian,
Mawgan Porth, Nr Newquay, Cornwall. 01637 860437
Water: Boat and Shore Fishing Trips
Species: Over 30 Species caught in 1996

Restorick
Contact: Trever Ridd. 29 Trebarwith Cresent, Newquay, Cornwall.
01637 878696
Water: Deep sea wreck and reef fishing.
Charges: 1/2 day trips 10 a.m. - 2 p.m. & 2 p.m. - 6 p.m. £10, All
day trips 9.30 a.m. - 5.30 p.m. £20, Conger fishing 6 p.m. - 9 p.m.
£7.50.
Season: All trips subject to sea conditions.
Methods: Full range of safety equipment including childrens life
jackets.

Thresher
Contact: Dixie Dean. 36 Lodeneck Avenue, Padstow, Cornwall.

Treyarnon Angling Centre
Contact: Ed Schliffke. Treyarnon Bay, St Merryn, Padstow, Cornwall.
01841 521157
Water: Shore Fishing Trips

How things Change!

A personal view by Malcolm Gilbert of Ammo Baits

As a youngster growing up in Helston (West Cornwall) during the 50s and 60s, the angling 'bug' dominated my entire world. The River Cober which runs into the Loe pool from the high moors between Redruth and Helston was my favourite haunt with occasional forays to fish in the streams at Gweek, Poltesco (Ruan Minor) or Binnerton (Helston side of Leedstown).

These streams, often no more than a few feet in width and inches deep, all held good numbers of wild brown trout. Fish of nine and ten inches were regularly caught and occasional three quarter pound trout made it to the grill pan. My largest ever was a monster of two and a quarter pounds taken on a grass hopper from the Cober where it runs alongside Helston boating lake. The boating lakes were full of eels and one year the authorities, in their wisdom, decided to introduce a stock of three quarter pound rainbow trout to control the weed which was impeding the oars of the rowing boats. I regret to say that the 'NO FISHING' signs failed to stop us once the park keeper had gone home. The temptation proved too much and I believe I can say with absolute confidence that within forty eight hours of their introduction, none remained.

Sometimes my father or a family friend would take me sea fishing and the pollock or wrasse were always obliging. I can even remember a late evening angling foray to a local beach whilst the family enjoyed a barbecue and I caught a couple of bass on my trout rod.

During the early seventies I returned to Cornwall after a few years spent in Birmingham and took up sea angling seriously. Some of my friends had been sea angling for many years and were already aware of deteriorating fish stocks but it seemed pretty good to me with predictable seasons for the various species and very few blanks. Charter boats were producing huge catches of pollock and ling from the off shore wrecks. The inshore sandbanks off West Cornwall still produced large turbot and blonde rays. Shore anglers enjoyed sizeable bass in the autumn with plenty of other species to ring the changes such as dabs, flounder, small eyed rays and plaice. Specimen hunters sought and sometimes caught the double figure (over ten pounds) pollock from either Logan Rock or Bosigran near Pendeen. It was all taken for granted and tourists would take advantage of the sport alongside the locals.

At this time, coarse angling was virtually unheard of in Cornwall. Between the mid seventies and the mid eighties, however, the situation changed dramatically. The provision of coarse angling venues began to take off and by the late eighties there were scores of lakes and ponds (many newly created) stocked with a variety of coarse fish imported into the county. Tourists came in numbers to take advantage and increasing numbers of residents started to take an interest in coarse angling.

At sea however things were deteriorating rapidly. The use of monofilament netting became vary widespread amongst the commercial fishing fleet. The daylight fishing ability of these nets combined with their relative cheapness led to gillnetting areas where tide and hitchy grounds had historically prevented netting. The fact that even in their wet state they weighed far less than the previous twisted nylon nets meant that even thirty five foot inshore vessels were able to carry almost twenty miles of nets. Hydraulic net haulers were developed to work the gear more efficiently. When these new nets were combined with modern fish location and accurate navigation electronics the increase in fish landings led to yet more boats turning to monofilament netting resulting in record landings pushing Newlyn to the top of the league tables. As fish became scarcer so the gillnetters resorted to using yet more netting to catch enough to remain viable. Larger boats (often

Sea

*Steve Ace with a beauty from Salcombe.
Picture - Veals*

grant aided) were acquired in order to go further afield and to carry more fishing gear so as to catch enough fish to remain in operation. An uncontrolled spiralling effort on a finite resource is of course unsustainable.

The resulting scarcity of fish led to some sea anglers who had enjoyed the days of plenty, giving up. Some even took up coarse angling where fish were undeniably present.

Sea angling is of course still a popular sport. There are still fish to be caught and in any case angling is not only about catching fish. The scenery - getting away from the crowds - the therapeutic surge of the surf are all part of sea angling. However, fish are scarcer and smaller than they once were. If sea fish stocks can be conserved and returned to their former levels the potential for a huge recreational industry supporting thousands of jobs in those coastal areas that need them and often at precisely the time of year which would lengthen the season, is enormous.

The political debate on over fishing throughout Europe is warming up and eventually we may see action following what as yet is only talk and the debate so far has not even considered the effect over fishing has had on the recreational sea angling industry. In other countries fisheries management takes account of recreational sea fishing both In biological and economic terms. Some species are actually managed for recreational fishing where research shows that the resource provides more economic activity as a sport fish. Anglers require licences and there are bag limits, size limits and seasonal controls. The essential research which enables quality management for sustainability and the enforcement of that management legislation is paid for with the licence income. Not a far cry from the concept adopted for management of our own wild game fisheries.

Why the vision of a substantial and sustainable recreational sea fishery has not attracted the interest of coastal tourism authorities in Europe is something of a mystery but the Republic of Ireland have introduced legislation to prohibit commercial fishing for bass, along with a two fish bag limit, because they recognise the economic potential in attracting bass anglers. Where this concept has existed in the U.S.A. for some years, the results have been a dramatic improvement in the stock and an ensuing sustainable increase in the value of the recreational fishery now calculated in billions of dollars:

The Cornish Federation of Sea Anglers

The C.F.C.A is a practical federation of Cornish sea angling clubs, elected to act in the interest of them all, to make representations to the appropriate authorities on their behalf and to further the sport of sea angling. Juniors and seniors of all races and creeds are welcome.

Although small by comparison to some other federations its reputation and influence on matters related to sea angling in Cornish waters is steadily becoming more recognised. In the field of conservation the federation is involved in continuing surveys into protection of bass and takes an active part, via its conservation officer, in the bass tagging programme. It also takes an active role in investigations regarding the effect of bait collecting on peeler crabs, rag and lug worm.

Pollution, ranging from litter left at fishing marks on the one hand to sewage outfalls and oil spillage on the other, is another topic in which the federation takes a lively interest.

We send out a monthly newsletter, have two general meetings and an AGM every year and a presentation/dinner/dance in March. We are a very friendly federation and always welcome new members, whether they be clubs or personal members.

For more details write to the secretary: Mrs Camilla Perry, 7 Henwood Crescent, St Columb Minor, Newquay, Cornwall TR7 3HG

Sea

Carl Emmery, aged 13, with a 12lb 8oz Bass. The best from the north coast in the summer of 1997.
Variety Sports

The Directory

and how to use it.

The directory has been divided up into Devon and Cornwall and North and South Wessex geographic areas as shown by the map on page 6. These three sections are sub divided into river fishing, stillwater trout and stillwater coarse fisheries.

Many associations, particularly in the Wessex regions, offer both game and coarse fishing on many different rivers and lakes. Each association entry gives briefs details of the fishing on offer.

Each section starts with river fishing and includes a short description of the rivers, canals etc. within the area. This section is sorted by river catchment area.

Stillwater coarse and stillwater trout fisheries are sorted alphabetically under their nearest town. Where coarse and game fishing is offered the entry will be cross referenced.

There is a river map on pages 70-71.

DEVON & CORNWALL
RIVER FISHING

AVON

South Devon stream not to be confused with Hampshire Avon or Bristol Avon. Rises on Dartmoor and enters sea at Bigbury. Brown trout, sea trout and salmon.

AXE

This quiet meandering stream rises in the hills of west Dorset, runs along the boundary with Somerset before flowing past Axminster to the sea at Seaton. The Axe is a fertile river with good trout fishing and a run of salmon and sea trout. The two main tributaries, the Coly and Yarty, are also trout streams and the Yarty has a good run of sea trout.

Stillwaters

See under stillwater trout, Honiton. One sea trout rod on River Axe.

Higher Cownhayne Farm

Contact: Mrs Pady, Higher Cownhayne Farm, Cownhayne Lane, Colyton, Devon, 01297 552267 Water: Fishing on River Coly. Species: Brown & Sea Trout. Charges: On application. Methods: Fly fishing, No netting.

CAMEL

The Camel rises on the north west edge of Bodmin Moor and flows past Camelford to its estuary at Wadebridge. The run of salmon tends to be late with some of the best fishing in November and December. Sea trout in summer. Also moorland brown trout fishing.

Bodmin Anglers Association

Contact: R Burrows, 26 Meadow Place, Bodmin, Cornwall 01208 75513 Water: 11.5 Miles on River Camel, 0.25 miles on River Fowey. Species: Salmon, Sea Trout. Permits: Roger Lashbrook at Stan Mays Garage, Bodmin. D.Odgers, Gwendreath, Dunmere, Bodmin. Charges: 1st May - 30th Sept £12 per day or £40 per week. 1st Oct - 30th Nov £25 per day. Season: Visitors permits May 1 - Nov 30. Methods: Fly, Worm, Spinner.

Butterwell

Contact: Tyson & Janet Jackson, Butterwell, Nr Nanstallon, Bodmin, Cornwall 01208 831515 Water: 1.5 miles River Camel. Species: Sea trout & Salmon. Charges: £18 per day, Maximum 5 rods per day. Season: 1st May - 30th August, night fly fishing only for Sea trout. 1st September - 15th December. Methods: Any method for Salmon.

Lifton Hall Country House Hotel

See entry under Teign.

Liskeard & District Angling Club

See entry under Lynher.

Wadebridge & Dist. Angling Association

Contact: Mr B. Brebner, 101 Egloshayle, Road, Wadebridge, 01208 813863 Water: 10 miles River Camel, 1 mile River Allen. Species: Salmon, Sea trout. Permits: Day / Week permits, Bait Bunker, Polmorla Road, Wadebridge. Charges: Day £15, Week £45. Season: Visitor permits end 1st November. Methods: No maggots, Artificial bait on some beats.

DART

Deep in the fastnesses of lonely Dartmoor rise the East and West Dart. Between their separate sources and Dartmeet, where they join these two streams and their tributaries are mainly owned by the Duchy of Cornwall and provide many miles of salmon, sea trout and trout fishing for visitors. The scenery is on the grand scale and the sense of freedom enjoyed when you know that you can fish away over miles and miles of river is seldom realised on this crowded island. This is a moorland fishery - swift flowing, boulder strewn, usually crystal clear.

Below Dartmeet the river rushes through a spectacular wooded valley before breaking out of the moor near Buckfastleigh and flowing on to its estuary at Totnes. Although there are brown trout throughout the river, these middle and lower reaches are primarily salmon and sea trout waters.

Buckfastleigh

Contact: S.W.W. Leisure Services, Higher Coombepark, Lewdown, Okehampton EX20

4QT 01837 871565 Water: 1/4 mile on River Dart. Austins Bridge to Nursery Pool Species: Salmon & Sea Trout Permits: From Leisure Services Charges: Season - £65. Limit of 16 rods.

Duchy Of Cornwall

Water: East & West Dart Rivers and its tributaries down to Dartmeet. Species: Salmon and Trout. Permits: The Arundell Arms, Lifton; Badgers Holt Ltd, Dartmeet; Charles Bingham (Fishing) Ltd, Whitchurch; James Bowden & Sons, Chagford; Brailey's Field Sports, Market St, Exeter; Drum Sports, Newton Abbot; Exeter Angling Centre, Smythen St, Exeter; The Forest Inn, Hexworthy, Poundsgate; Holne Chase Hotel, Ashburton; Mabins News, Fore St, Buckfastleigh; Post Office Stores, Postbridge, Yelverton; Poundsgate Shop, Poundsgate, Newton Abbot; Prince Hall Hotel, Two Bridges, Princetown; Princetown Post Office; South West Tackle Developments, Paignton; Two Bridges Hotel, Princetown; Charges: Salmon Season: £125, Week £70, Day £20. Trout Season: £55, Week £15, Day £4. Methods: Fly only. Additional information on permit.

ERME

A small Devon stream rising on Dartmoor and flowing south through Ivybridge to the sea. The Erme is probably best known for its sea trout, but there is also a run of salmon and brown trout are present throughout its length.

EXE AND TRIBUTARIES

The Exe rises high on Exmoor and flows through open moorland until it plunges into a steep wooded valley near Winsford. By the time Tiverton is reached the valley has widened and from here to the sea the Exe meanders through a broad pastoral vale until it flows into the estuary near Exeter and finally into the sea between Exmouth and Dawlish Warren. It is the longest river in the south west.

Throughout most of its length the Exe is a good trout stream, the fast flowing, rocky upper reaches abounding in fish of modest average size, which increases as the river becomes larger and slower in its middle and lower reaches, where fish approaching a pound feature regularly in the daily catch. The Exe has a good run of salmon and some fishing can be obtained on hotel waters in the middle reaches. In the deep slow waters around Exeter there is a variety of coarse fish, as there is in the Exeter Ship Canal which parallels the river from Exeter to the estuary at Topsham. In an area noted for its sea trout streams, the Exe is unusual in that it has no appreciable run of sea trout, but it does have some grayling, a species not often found in the south west. The two main tributaries - the Barle and the Culm - could not be more different in character. The Barle is a swift upland stream which rises high on Exmoor not far from the source of the Exe, and runs a parallel course, first through open moor and then through a picturesque wooded valley, before joining the parent river near Dulverton. it has good trout fishing throughout and salmon fishing on the lower reaches.

The Culm issues from the Blackdown Hills and in its upper reaches is a typical dry fly trout stream, with good hatches of fly and free-rising fish. From Cullompton until it joins the Exe, the Culm becomes a coarse fishery, with the dace in particular of good average size.

Bridge House Hotel
Contact: Brian Smith, Bridge House Hotel, Bampton, Devon EX16 9NF 01398 331298 Water: 1 Mile on River Exe. Species: Salmon & Trout. Permits: As above. Charges: Salmon £20 per day, Trout £10 per day. Season: March 15th - Sept 30th. Methods: Fly, occasional spinner.
Broford Fishing
Contact: P. Veale, Lance Nicholson Fishing Tackle & Guns, 9 High Street, Dulverton, Somerset 01398 323409 Water: Approx 5 miles bank fishing on Little Exe. Species: Wild Brown Trout with occasional Salmon. Permits: As above. Charges: £10 per day. Season: 15th March - 30th September. Methods: Fly Only.
Carnarvon Arms Hotel
Contact: Dulverton, Somerset TA22 9AE 01398 323302 Water: Fishing on Rivers Exe & Barle Species: Salmon & Wild Brown Trout. Charges: Please Telephone for details.
Environment Agency Exe and Creedy
Contact: 01392 444000 Water: 3 Miles; 4 sections between Cowley Bridge and Countess Wear Bridge. Species: Salmon. Permits: Season and Day permits - Exeter Angling Centre, Smythen Street, Off City Arcade, Fore Street, Exeter. (Tel: 01392 436404). Day permits - Topp Tackle, 63 Station Road, Taunton; Country Sports, 9 William Street, Tiverton; The Enviroment Agency, Manley House, Exeter. Charges: Season (Limited) £40, Day £4. Season: 1st June - 30th September. Methods: Fly or spinning.
Half Stone Sporting Agency
Contact: Mr Roddy Rae, 6 Hescane Park, Cheriton Bishop, Devon EX6 6SP 01647 24643 Water: 2 miles River Exe divided into 3 beats, 2 rods per beat per day plus 1.5 miles on River Teign Species: Salmon, Brown Trout & Grayling on the Exe. Salmon Sea Trout & Brown Trout on River Teign. Charges: Exe - £30 day, Teign - £20 per day. Season: Exe: 14th Feb - 30th September. Teign: 1st Feb - 30th September Methods: Fly & Spinning.
Hatswell
Contact: Mrs B.A.Macdonald, Hatswell, Lower Washfield, Tiverton, Devon EX16 9PE 01884 253016 Water: 600 yds, single bank on River Exe. Species: Salmon, Brown trout. Permits: Post Offices. Charges: Charges on application.
J.S.Sporting
Contact: John Sharpe, Greenwells, East Anstey, Tiverton, Devon EX16 9JU 01398 341379 Water: 2 miles Upper Exe and

Haddeo. Species: Trout & occasional Salmon. Permits: From above address. Charges: £12.50 per day. Season: As per Enviroment Agency seasons. Methods: Trout - Fly only, Salmon - Fly & Spinning.
Lifton Hall Country House Hotel
See entry under Teign.
Tarr Steps Hotel
Contact: Shaun or Sue Blackmore, Tarr Steps Hotel, Hawkridge, Dulverton, Somerset TA22 9PY 01643 851293 Water: 3.5 Miles double bank on River Barle. Species: Wild Brown Trout, Salmon. Charges: From £10 per day Trout, From £15 per day Salmon. Methods: Trout; Fly only, Salmon; Fly and spinner when water is coloured.
Tiverton Fly Fishing Association
Contact: Exe Valley Angling, 19 Westexe South, Tiverton, Devon EX16 5DQ 01884 242275 Water: 3.5 Miles on River Exe. Species: Trout & Grayling. Charges: Senior £12, Conc. £4, Guests £5. Season: 15th March - 30th September. Methods: Fly only.

FOWEY
Rises near the highest point of Bodmin Moor from which it flows south, then turns to the west, and finally south again through Lostwithiel to its long estuary. A late salmon river. Also good sea trout fishing and some trout fishing.

Bodmin Anglers Association
See entry under Camel. 0.25 miles River Fowey.
Lanhydrock Angling Association
Contact: Brian Nuelaner, The National Trust, Regional Office, Lanhydrock, Bodmin, Cornwall PL30 4DE 01208 74281 Water: 2 miles on River Fowey. Species: Sea trout, Salmon. Charges: £10 Daily, £25 Weekly (maximum 6 tickets daily). Season: 1st April - 30th September. Methods: Artificial bait only.
Lifton Hall Country House Hotel
See entry under Teign.
Fowey Liskeard & District Angling Club
See entry under Lynher.
Lostwithiel Fishing Association
Contact: F.H.Cox, 6 Cott Road, Lostwithiel, Cornwall 01208 872136 Water: 2 miles water, Both banks, River Fowey. Species: Salmon, Sea trout, Brown trout. Permits: Rogers Tackle Shop, Bodmin. Tackle Shop, Lostwithiel. Charges: £55 per season, £30 per week, £10 per day. Season: 1st April - 15th December. Methods: All baits.

LOOE
The twin rivers, East and West Looe, have their sources near Liskeard and join shortly before reaching the sea at Looe. Although small, there is a run of sea trout, and brown trout throughout.

LYN
Chalk Water, Weir Water, Oare Water, Badgeworthy Water - these are the streams that tumble down from the romantic Doone

Country of Exmoor and join to form the East Lyn, which cascades through the spectacular wooded ravine of the National Trust's Watersmeet Estate. The main river has good runs of salmon and sea trout, and wild brown trout teem on the Lyn and the tributary streams.

Environment Agency Watersmeet and Glenthorne
Contact: 01392 444000 Water: The fishery is in two parts. The fishery leased by the E.A. from the National Trust - Tors Road, Lynmouth to Woodside Bridge, right bank only; Woodside Bridge to Watersmeet both banks; upstream of the Watersmeet right bank only to Rockford. The Glenthorne Fishery - right bank only upstream of Rockford to 300 yards downstream of Brendon Road Bridge. Half a mile of Trout fishing is available on the Hoaroak Water between Hillsford Bridge and Watersmeet; this is specifically for children, who only require a Trout rod licence when fishing this particular stretch if they are aged 12 years or over. Care should be taken as the rocks are slippery. Species: Salmon, Sea Trout, Brown Trout. Permits: Mr & Mrs Hillier, Brendon Houes Hotel, Brendon. Mrs M Mirow, Lynmouth Post Office, 20 Lynmouth St., Lynmouth. Tourist Information Centre, Town Hall, Lynton; Mrs.J.Fenell, Variety Sports, 23 Broad Street, Ilfracombe; Mrs Topp, Topp Tackle, 63 Station Road, Taunton. Charges: Salmon & Sea Trout, season withdrawn for conservation reasons, week £35, day £13.50, evening (8 p.m. to 2 a.m.) £4; Brown Trout, season £27.50, week £10, day £3. Bag Limits: 2 salmon, 6 sea trout, 8 brown trout. Season: Salmon 1st March - 30th September; Sea Trout & Trout 15th March - 30th September.Fishing permitted 8 a.m. to sunset, except from 1st June - 30th September when fishing by traditional fly fishing methods is permitted until 2 a.m. between Tors Road & Rockford. Methods: Brown Trout, Fly only. Salmon, No shrimp or prawn. No worm or maggot before 1st June. No weight may be used whilst fly fishing. The weight used for worm fishing and spinning must be lead free and not weigh more than 0.5 ounce and must be attached at least 18 inches from the hook.

LYNHER
Rises on Bodmin Moor and joins the Tamar estuary opposite Plymouth. Brown trout and runs of salmon and sea trout.

Liskeard & District Angling Club
Contact: Bill Elliot (Hon Sec), 64 Portbyhan Road, West Looe, Cornwall PL13 2QN 01503 264173 Water: 26 Miles of Rivers Lynher, Fowey, Camel, Inny, Seaton River, West Looe River. Species: Salmon & Sea trout. Permits: Tremar Tropicals shop, Liskeard. Lashbrooks Tackle, Bodmin. Lostwithiel Angling Centre, Lostwithiel. Looe Tropicals & Pets, East Looe. Osborne & Cragg Tackle, Plymouth Barbican. Watson

Hairdressing, Callington. Post Office, Rilla Mill. Homeleigh Garden Centre, Launceston. Charges: Adult day Ticket £12.50, Adult weekly ticket £37.50. Season: River Lynher; 1st March - 14th October. River Fowey 1st April - 14th October. River Camel 1st May - 14th October. Methods: Artificials only on some beats on River Fowey.

MENALHYL

Small stream starting near St Columb Major and entering the sea north of Newquay. Brown trout fishing.

OTTER

The Otter springs to life in the Blackdown Hills and flows through a broad fertile valley to join the sea near the little resort of Budleigh Salterton. This is primarily a brown trout stream noted for its dry fly fishing for trout of good average weight. There is also some sea trout fishing in the lower reaches.

Clinton Devon Estates
Water: 1.5 miles on the River Otter from Clamour Bridge (footpath below Otterton) to White Bridge near Budleigh Salterton. Species: Brown Trout Charges: Free to EA rod licence holders Season: 15 March to 31 October.
Deer Park Hotel
Contact: Reception Deer Park Hotel, Weston, Nr Honiton, Devon EX14 OPG 01404 41266 Water: 6 miles on River Otter, 1 mile on Coly Species: Brown Trout, Occasional Sea Trout & Salmon Charges: Day or season permits available. Prices on application Season: 15th March - 30th September Methods: Dry Fly only.

PLYM

A short stream rising on Dartmoor and running into Plymouth Sound. Trout fishing on the Plym and its tributary the Meavy, with some sea trout on the lower reaches and a late run of salmon.

Plymouth & Dist Freshwater Angling Assoc
Contact: Mr D.L.Owen, 39 Burnett Road, Crownhill, Plymouth PL6 5BH 01752 705033 Water: 1 Mile of River Plym, 1.5 miles on River Tavy. Species: Salmon, Sea Trout, Brown Trout. Permits: Snowbee, Parkway Industrial Estate, St Modwen Road, Plymouth. D.K.Sports, 88 Vauxhall Street, Plymouth. Charges: £10 a day Monday to Friday up to 30th September incl. £15 a day Monday to Friday from 1st October. Season: April - 15th December (Plym). Methods: Artificial baits only.
Tavy,Walkham & Plym Fishing Club
See entry under Tavy.

SEATON

Short stream to the east of Looe with fishing for brown trout.

TAMAR

The Tamar rises near the north coast, and for most of its course forms the boundary between Devon and Cornwall. It is always a lowland stream flowing through farmland and this fact is reflected in the size of its trout which have a larger average size than the acid moorland streams. Around Launceston, the Tamar is joined by five tributaries - Ottery, Carey, Wolf, Thrushel and Lyd - which offer good trout fishing, as does the Inny which enters a few miles downstream. There is a good run of salmon and sea trout, the latter being particularly numerous on the Lyd. There are also grayling in places.

Arundell Arms
Contact: Mrs Anne Voss-Bark, Lifton, Devon PL16 OAA 01566 784666 Water: 20 miles on River Tamar and its tributaries Species: Salmon, Sea Trout and Brown Trout Charges: Please telephone for details.
Bude Angling Association
Contact: Mr L.Bannister, 2 Creathorn Road, Bude EX23 8NT 01288 352476 Water: 3 miles upper reach of the River Tamar. Species: Brown trout (Wild). Permits: Bude Angling Supplies, Queen Street, Bude. Homeleigh Garden Centre, Dutson, Launceston. Charges: £3 day, Week tickets available. Season: March 15th - Sept 30th. Methods: Fly only.
Endsleigh Fishing Club
Contact: Mr D.Bradbury, Endsleigh House, Milton Abbot, Tavistock, Devon PL19 OPQ Water: River Tamar. Species: Salmon & Sea trout. Charges: Per rod per day, £20 March - April, £30 May, £28 June, £20 July - August, £48 Sept - Oct. Methods: Fly.
Launceston Anglers Association
Contact: Colin Hookway, 7 Grenville Park, Yelverton, Devon 01822 855053 Water: 6 miles on River Tamar + Carey, 4 miles River Inney Species: Brown Trout, Sea Trout, Salmon. Permits: Only from Homeleigh Garden Centre, Dutson, Launceston. Charges: Salmon & Sea Trout; Day £17.50, Week £45 to 31st August. Day £25, Week £55 from 1st September. Brown Trout: Day £7.50, Week £25, Juniors £2 a day. Day tickets valid for 24 hours from time of purchase. Season: From 1st September - 31st August. Methods: Brown trout - fly only, Salmon & Sea trout - any method subject to byelaws.
Lifton Hall Country House Hotel
See entry under Teign.

TAVY

This noted salmon and sea trout river rises deep in Dartmoor and flows its rocky course through Tavistock to its estuary, which joins that of the Tamar to the north of Plymouth. The main tributary is the Walkham, which also rises on Dartmoor and provides good moorland trout fishing.

Plymouth & Dist Freshwater Angling Assoc
See entry under Plym

Tavy,Walkham & Plym Fishing Club

Contact: Ian.H.Parker, Oakhaven, 36 Upland Drive, Derriford, Plymouth PL6 6BD 01752 787058 Water: Rivers Tavy, Walkham, Plym, Meavy. Species: Brown Trout, Salmon, Sea Trout. Permits: Only through D.K.Sports, Barbican, Plymouth. Barkells, Duke St, Tavistock. Moorland Garage, Yelverton. Charges: Season Trout £40, Season Salmon / Sea trout £100, plus other permits. Please phone above No. for details. Season: See Environment Agency season dates. Please note, no day tickets after 30th September. Methods: No worm, prawn, shrimp on Club permit waters.

TAW

Like the neighbouring Torridge, the Taw is a salmon and sea trout stream with several hotel waters, offering the visiting angler the opportunities to fish on many miles of river. The Taw quickly leaves Dartmoor after rising close to Okehampton and flows through the rolling farmland of north Devon to its estuary at Barnstaple. Its main tributary, the Mole, also has good salmon and sea trout fishing, and the Mole's own main tributary, the Bray, is a good little trout stream.

Crediton Fly Fishing Club
See entry under Yeo. 1.5 miles River Taw
Fox & Hounds Hotel
Contact: Mr J Pitts, Eggesford, Chulmleigh, Devon EX18 7JZ 01769 580345 Water: Fishing on Rivers Taw & Little Dart. Species: Prime Salmon, Sea Trout & Brown Trout. Charges: Prime Salmon & Sea Trout £20 per day (24 hrs), 1/2 day £12, Brown Trout £10.50 day. Salmon, Trout and Sea Trout full week permit (7 days) £100. Season: 1st April - 30th September.
Highbullen Hotel
Contact: Chris Taylor, Chittlehamholt, Umberleigh, Devon EX37 9HD 01769 540561 Water: 3 miles River Mole & 5 miles River Taw Species: Salmon, Sea Trout & Brown Trout Season: Salmon, Sea Trout 1st March - 30th September, Brown Trout 14th march - 30th September Methods: Spinner March & April. Fly March & September.
Lifton Hall Country House Hotel
See entry under Teign.
Rising Sun Water
Contact: Peter Huntington, Hobbs Wood Cottage, Charles Brayford, Barnstaple EX32 7PY 01598 760430 Water: 2.75 Miles River Taw. Species: Salmon, Sea Trout, Brown Trout. Charges: £25 per day 06.00 - 06.00. Season: 1st March - 30th September. Methods: March - April Fly / Spinning, May - September Fly only.

TEIGN

The Teign has two sources high up on Dartmoor which form the North and South Teign but the two branches of the Teign quickly leave the moor to join west of Chagford while still very small streams. Between Chagford and Steps Bridge the river runs through a dramatic wooded gorge which is at its most spectacular at Fingle Bridge, a popular beauty spot. All along the Teign the Spring fisherman is greeted by myriads of daffodils, which are at their most numerous around Clifford Bridge. The upper Teign offers good fishing for wild trout and sea trout, with salmon fishing in suitable conditions from April to the end of the season. Much of the upper river is controlled by the Upper Teign Fishing Association. From just south of the Moretonhampstead - Exeter road to the estuary at Newton Abbot. the Teign is mostly controlled by the Lower Teign Fishing Association. This water has plenty of brown trout but is essentially a sea trout and salmon fishery.

Lifton Hall Country House Hotel
Contact: Lifton Hall Country House Hotel, New Road, Lifton, Devon PL16 0DR 01566 784263 Water: Private beats on - Teign, Camel, Exe, Taw, Tamar, Fowey. Species: Brown Trout, Salmon, Sea Trout. Charges: Rod fees from £10 - £25 per day, With ghillies from £110 - £120 per day.

Lower Teign Fishing Association
Contact: Mr R Waters, 121 Topsham Road, Exeter, Devon Water: 14 miles River Teign. Species: Salmon, Sea Trout. Permits: Drum Sports, Newton Abbot. 3 Beats with 3 tickets on each (beat 3 not available until 1st May). Season: 1st Febuary - 30th September. Methods: Spinning, fly (fly only at night), No worming or maggots.

Mill End Hotel
Contact: Julian Peck, Mill End Hotel, Sandy Park, Chagford, Devon TQ13 8JN 01647 432282 Water: Fishing on River Teign Species: Salmon, Brown trout, Sea trout. Permits: Chagford Post Office, Anglers Rest and from Hotel Reception.

Upper Teign Fishing Association.
Contact: Mr JTH Getliff 22 The Square Chagford Devon TQ13 8AB 01647 433493 Water: Approx 8 miles on upper Teign. Species: Brown Trout, Sea Trout & Salmon. Permits: From: The Anglers Rest, Drewsteignton. Bowdens, Chagford. Drum Sports, Newton Abbot. Mill End Hotel, Sandy Park, Chagford. Clifford Bridge Caravan Park. Braileys Field Centre, Exeter. Exeter Angling Centre. Charges: Ordinary Member - Annual Subscription £140 Full season for Salmon, Sea Trout & Brown Trout. Trout Member - Annual subscription £50 Full season for Brown Trout. Temporary Members' Tickets - Salmon & Sea Trout £15 per day (7 ticket limit per day from Anglers Rest). Sea Trout £6 per day (4 ticket limit per day from Bowdens, Chagford). Membership Enquiries to Secretary. Brown Trout Adult season £35, juvenille (under 16) £12. Week £15. juvenille £6. Day £4. juvenille £2. Season: Brown Trout: March 15th - September 30th. Sea Trout: March 15th - September 30th. Salmon: February 1st - September 30th.

TORRIDGE

Throughout its length the Torridge flows through the rolling farmland of north Devon. It rises close to the coast near the Cornish

border and swings in a great arc before flowing into the estuary that it shares with the Taw. The middle and lower reaches are best known for its salmon and sea trout, but can offer surprisingly good trout fishing. The upper reaches offer good small-stream trout fishing, as does the main tributary, the Okement, which is formed by two branches that rise on Dartmoor to the south of Okehampton.

Clinton Arms
Contact: Roy Laney, Frithelstock, Torrington, Devon 01805 623279 Water: Approx half mile of double bank on River Torridge (left hand bank only last 200yds). Species: Brown trout, Sea trout, Salmon. Charges: £100 day rod for season, £12.50 day rod. Season: Tuesday, Wednesday, Thursday.

Half Moon Fishery
Contact: Charles Inniss, Half Moon Hotel, Sheepwash, Nr Hatherleigh, North Devon 01409 231376 Water: 10 Miles on R.Torridge + 6 Acre lake. Species: River; Salmon, Sea Trout, Brown Trout. Lake; Rainbows only. Charges: Lake; £14 - 4 Fish, £8.50 - 2 Fish. River; Salmon £18, Sea Trout £12, Brown Trout £8. Season: March 1st - October 31st. Methods: Fly only.

Little Warham Fishery
Contact: Group Captain P. Norton-Smith, Little Warham House, Beaford, Winkleigh, Devon 01805 603317 Water: 2 Miles of River Torridge. Species: Salmon, Sea Trout, Brown Trout. Permits: As above Charges: £18 per day per rod, All species. Season: March 1st - September 30th. Methods: Fly only.

Simon Gawesworth School of Fly Fishing
Contact: Simon Gawesworth, 95 New Street, Torrington, Devon EX38 8BT 01805 623256 Water: 10 Miles of fine Salmon, Sea Trout and Trout. Permits: Beats available on day ticket. Charges: Brown Trout from £8, Sea Trout from £12, Salmon from £15 per rod per day. Season: 1st March (Salmon) 15th March (Sea trout & Brown Trout) through to 30th September inc. Methods: Fly only after 30th April.

South Hay Fishery
See entry under stillwater trout, Beaworthy. 2 miles on Torridge.

YEALM

Upper Yealm Fishery
Contact: Gerald Hoskins, Devon 01752 772482 Water: 1 Mile both banks River Yealm. Species: Sea Trout, Brown Trout (Stocked), Salmon. Permits: Snowbee, Parkway Industrial Estate, St Modwen Road, Plymouth. Charges: Full membership £100, Half rod £50, Day ticket (All species) £10. Season: Brown Trout & Sea Trout 15th March - 30th Sept, Salmon 1st April - 15th December. Methods: Fly Fishing & Spinning.

YEO

Crediton Fly Fishing Club
Contact: David Pope, 21 Creedy Road, Crediton EX17 1EW 01363 773557 Water: 5 miles Rivers Yeo & Creedy, 1.5 miles River

Taw. Species: Brown Trout, Sea Trout & Salmon. Permits: Contact on the internet: http://freespace.virgin.net/howard.thresher/cffcl.html Charges: Weekly (5 days) £20, Season £55, Juniors £5. Season: Environment Agency Season. Methods: Fly only.

STILLWATER TROUT

BARNSTAPLE
Blakewell Fisheries
Contact: Mr Richard & John Nickell, Blakewell Fisheries, Muddiford, Barnstaple, Devon, EX31 4ET, 01271 344533, Water: 4.5 Acre Lake. Species: Rainbow, Brown & Brook Trout. Charges: 5 Fish £20, 4 Fish £16, 3 Fish £14, 2 Fish £12. Season: All Year. Methods: Fly Only.

BEAWORTHY
Half Moon Fishery
Water: See entry under Torridge. 6 acre trout lake.

Kingslake
Contact: Mr & Mrs King, Kingslake, Chilla, Beaworthy, Devon. 01409 231401, Water: 1.8 Acre Lake, Species: Rainbow Trout. Charges: Day ticket £14 (4 fish), Half day £10 (2 fish). Season: Open all year. Methods: Fly fishing, Max four rods.

South Hay Fishery
Contact: Mr & Mrs David Kirby, South Barn Farm, South Hay, Shebbear, Beaworthy 01409 281857, Water: 2 acre Trout lake, 2 Miles of River Torridge. Species: Rainbow Trout (lake), Brown Trout, Sea Trout, Salmon (river). Charges: Lake £5 per day plus £1.50 per lb, River £10 per day. Season: Lake - all year, River - Mid March to End September. Methods: Fly only.

BIDEFORD
Clifford Farm Estate
Contact: Woolfardisworthy, Nr Bideford, North Devon EX39 5RB, 01237 431319, Water: Small well established lake, Species: Trout, Charges: On application.

Fosfelle Country House Hotel
Contact: Hartland, Bideford, Devon 01237 441273, Water: Pond approx 1/2 acre. Species: Rainbow & Golden Trout. Charges: £7.50 1/2 day - 2 Trout. Season: Open all year. Methods: Displayed on site.

Torridge Valley Trout Farm
Contact: Mr Limb, Halspill, Nr Weare Gifford, Bideford, Devon 01237 475797, Water: Small Lake. Species: Rainbow Trout. Charges: £3.50 to fish + fish at £1.75/lb. Season: 7 days week, 10am - 6pm. Methods: Any.

BODMIN
Fenwick Trout Fishery
Contact: David Thomas, Fenwick Trout Fishery, Old Coach Road, Denmere, Bodmin, Cornwall, PL31 2RD, 01208 78296, Water: 2 acre lake. Species: Rainbow 1.5lb - 12lb,

Browns to 10lb +. Charges: £18 Full day 5 fish, £9.50 Half day 2 fish, £10 Catch & Release. Season: All year. Methods: Barbless hooks, only for catch & release.

Temple Trout Fishery
Contact: Mr Julian Jones, Temple Trout Fishery, Temple Road, Temple, Bodmin, Cornwall 01208 850250, Water: 2.7 Acre lake. Species: Rainbows & Brown Trout. Permits: Available at fishery Tel: 01208 821730. Charges: Club membership £6 entitles members to 10% discount on tickets, to fish club events and to purchase a season ticket at £105 for 25 Trout. Full day £20, 5 fish. 3/4 day £17.50, 4 fish. 1/2 day £14, 3 fish. evening £10, 2 fish. child under 16 & disabled £10, 2 fish all day, extra fish £5.50. Season: Open all year round from 9 a.m to dusk, in winter open 3 days a week Wednesday, Thursday and Sundays or by appointment. Methods: Fly fishing.

BOSCASTLE

Venn Down Lakes
Contact: Ted & Sue Bowen, Trebowen, Trevalga, Boscastl. 01840 25001. Water: 2 pools, 3 acres. Species: Rainbow Trout. Charges: Ticket to fish £5, plus fish at £1.85 lb. Junior ticket £3 - 1 fish. Season: Open all year except xmas day. Methods: Max hook size 10, single fly only.

CULLOMPTON

Goodiford Mill Fishery
Contact: David Wheeler, Goodiford Mill, Kentisbeare, Cullompton, Devon, EX15 2AS, 01884 266233, Water: 2 Lakes in 4.5 acres. Species: Rainbow & Brown Trout. Charges: £18 x 4 fish, £15 x 3 fish, Evening £13 x 2 fish, £7 to fish & £1.60lb. Season: All year. Methods: Max 10 longshank.

FALMOUTH

Mylor Angling Lakes
Contact: Sue Palmer, Off Comfort Rd, Mylor Bridge, Falmouth 01326 373975, Water: 2 x 1 Acre Lakes. Species: Rainbow Trout. Permits: Only on site. Charges: £6.50 to fish + £1.75 per lb, Other tickets available. Methods: Fly fishing - rules published at lakes for sporting tickets.

HAYLE

Tree Meadow Trout Fishery
Contact: John Hodge, Tree Meadow, Deveral Road, Fraddam, Hayle 01736 850899, Water: Two lakes, 2.75 and 1 acre. Species: Rainbow and Brown trout. Permits: From fishery on (01736) 850583. Charges: Day ticket £7 plus £1.80 lb (first four fish killed then catch and release). Sporting ticket £15 all fish returned. Other tickets from £15 - £35. Season: Open all year 9 a.m. to dusk. Methods: Fly fishing, Barbless or debarbed hooks, No droppers, Hook size 10 max.

HOLSWORTHY

Mill Leat Trout Fishery
Contact: Mr Birkett, Thornbury, Holsworthy,

Devon 01409 261426, Water: Species: Rainbow Trout. Charges: £5 plus £1.50 per lb. No Limit. Season: 1st April - 31st October. Methods: Fly only.

HONITON

Hollies Trout Farm
Contact: Bobby Roles, Sheldon, Honiton, Devon EX14 0QS, 01404 841428, Water: Spring fed lake. Species: Rainbow & Brown Trout. Charges: Full day £19 - 4 fish, Half day £15 - 3 fish or £4.50 & £1.60lb. Concessions for OAP's and under 12's, Season: Open all year dawn to dusk. Methods: Dry & Wet fly only.

Otter Falls
Contact: John Wardell, Old Spurtham Farm, Upottery, Devon EX14 9QD, 01404 861634, Water: Two x 2 acre lakes. Species: Rainbow Trout. Permits: As above. Charges: £25 Full day, £15 Half day. Season: No season - phone first. Methods: Barbless hooks, No lures.

Stillwaters
Contact: Mr M.J.H.Ford, Lower Moorhayne Farm, Yarcombe, Nr Honiton 01404 861284, Water: 1 acre lake / 1 Sea trout rod on River Axe at the Sea Pool. Species: Trout & Sea Trout. Charges: From £10. Season: March 1st - November 1st. Methods: Fly only.

IVYBRIDGE

Mill Leat Trout Farm
Contact: Chris Trant, Ermington, Nr Ivybridge, Devon PL21 9NT, 01548 830172, Water: 3/4 Acre lake. Species: Rainbow Trout. Permits: No Environment Agency licence needed - we have a block licence. Charges: 2 fish £9, 4 fish £16 or £3 charge then £1.50lbs. Season: Open all year - booking advisable. Methods: No lures.

KINGSBRIDGE

Valley Springs
Contact: J Bishop, Sherford, Nr Kingsbridge, Devon 01548 531574, Water: 2 Lakes totalling approx 3 acres, Trout & Coarse. Species: Rainbow & Brown Trout. Charges: £7 per visit + £2 per lb. Season: Open all year. Methods: Barbless hooks, Traditional fly fishing methods only.

LAUNCESTON

Braggs Wood Trout Fishery
Contact: Braggs Wood Water, Braggs Hill, Boyton, Nr Launceston 01566 776474, Water: 1 Acre lake. Species: Rainbow & Brown Trout. Charges: 2 Fish ticket £11, 4 Fish ticket £19, Sporting ticket £5 + £1.60 per lb. Season: All year round 8 a.m. to dark. Methods: Max hook size 8.

Rose Park Fishery
Contact: Rose Park Fishery, Trezibbett, Altarnun, Nr Launceston 01566 86278, Water: Two lakes. Species: Rainbow, Wild & Stocked. Stocked Brown Trout. Permits: From the fishery. Charges: 1st fish £4 + £1.65lb. Thereafter each fish £1.65lb. All browns £2.05lb. Season: Open all year. Methods: Fly fishing.

NEWQUAY

Full Bag Fly Fishery
Contact: Adam Coad, Little Ellenglaze Farm, Cubert, Nr Newquay, Cornwall 01637 830839, Water: 2 Acres. Species: Rainbow Trout, Brown Trout. Charges: Full day £20, 5 Hours £12, Sporting full day £15, Sporting 5 Hours £10. Season: 1st March - 31st October. Opens 9 a.m. Methods: Fly only.

NEWTON ABBOT

Watercress Fishery
Contact: Mr Anthony Allen, Kerswell Springs, Chudleigh, Newton Abbot, Devon. TQ13 0DW, 01626 852168, Water: 3 spring fed lakes totalling approx 5 acres. New for 98 - Alder lake now stocked with Brown + Rainbow trout 1.5lb - 8lb. Species: Rainbow, Brown, Brook Trout. Charges: Day £20.50 - 5 fish max 8 hours. £18 4 fish. half day £15 3 fish. eve £10.75 2 fish. Alder lake (Brown + Brook) £9 full day, £7 half day. Season: Open all year. Methods: Hooks no longer than size 10 longshank. Alder lake - Catch & release, Dry fly or small nymph, Barbless hooks only.

PADSTOW

St. Merryn Fly Fishing Club
Contact: Hon. Sec. Bill Newcombe, 8 Coastguard Station, Hawkers Cove, Padstow 01841 533090, Water: 3 Acre Lake, Species: Rainbow Trout, Permits: Pig Trough Restaraunt, St. Merryn. Charges: £10 Half day. £20 Full day, Season: Methods: Barbless Hooks. No Boobies

PENZANCE

Drift Resevoir
Contact: T.B.Shorland (Bailiff), Drift Ways, Drift Resevoir, Penzance, Cornwall, TR19 6AB, 01736 363869, Water: 65 acre reservoir. Species: Stock Rainbows (3 per day 10 weekly) Wild Browns (No limits on Browns). Permits: At Bailiff's house on reservoir (also Environment Agency licences available). Charges: £100 season, £20 weekly, £7 day, £5 evening. Season: 1st April - 12th October Brown trout, 1st April - 31st October Rainbows. Methods: No static with boobies, any other traditional fly or lures.

PLYMOUTH

Drakelands
Contact: Mr Elford, Higher Drakelands, Hemerdon, Plympton, Plymouth, Devon 01752 344691, Water: 1.75 acre lake. Species: Brown Trout, Rainbow Trout. Charges: Ticket to fish £3 plus fish @ £1.85 lb, 1/2 day ticket £10 - 4 hrs (2 fish), £13.50 - 6 hrs (3 fish), £17 - 8 hrs (4 fish), £20 - 8 hrs (5 fish). Season: Open all year, Tuesday - Sunday. Methods: Barbless hooks only.

SALTASH

Bake Fishing Lakes
Contact: Chris Bond, Trerule Farm, Trerule Foot, Saltash, Cornwall 01503 240304, Water: 5 Lakes adding up to 14+ acres,

coarse and trout. Species: Rainbow and Brown Trout. Permits: Clives Tackle & Bait (Plymouth). Charges: 4 Fish £22, 3 Fish £17.50, 2 Fish £12 or £5 per day + £2 per lb, Catch and release £15 per day. Season: Autumn / Winter 8am - Dusk, Spring / Summer 7am - Dusk. Methods: Catch and release on one lake. Barbless, kill first two fish.

SEATON

Wiscombe Park Fishery
Contact: Mike Raynor, Wiscombe Park Fishery, Colyton, Devon EX13 6JE, 01404 871474, Water: Two 1/2 Acre lakes. Species: Rainbow Trout, Brown Trout. Permits: Self-sevice (No booking). Charges: £17 per day (8 fish limit), £12 per 4hrs (3 fish), £8.50 per 2 hrs (2 fish), Children (under 15) accompanied by permit holding adult free. Season: All year, Methods: Fly fishing (singles).

SOUTH BRENT

Somerswood Lake
Contact: S A Goodman, Brent Mill Farm, South Brent 01364 72154, Water: 2 acres in Avon valley. Species: Rainbow Trout. Charges: Full day £16 for 4 fish, 1/2 day £10 for 2 fish. Season: Open all year. Methods: Fly.

ST AUSTELL

Innis Fly Fishery
Contact: Mrs Pam Winch, Innis Fly Fishery Clubhouse, Innis Moor, Penwithick, St Austell, PL26 8YH, 01726 851162, Water: 15 Acres (3 Lakes), Stream fed enclosed water. Species: Rainbow trout. Permits: As above. Charges: Full day £18 (5 Fish), 1/2 day £9.50 (2 Fish) Catch + Release £10. Season: All year, 8.00 a.m. to dusk. Methods: Barbless hooks when catch & release.

TAVISTOCK

Tavistock Trout Farm & Fishery
Contact: Abigail Underhill, Parkwood Road, Tavistock, Devon Pl19 OJS, 01822 615441, Water: 5 Lakes totalling approx 4 acres. Species: Rainbow trout, Brown Trout. Charges: Full day 4 fish permit - Osprey Lake £30, Full day 4 fish Kingfisher + Heron £16.50. Season: Open all year 8am - dusk. Methods: Max hook size 10.

TIVERTON

Bellbrook Valley Trout Fishery
Contact: Mike Pusey, Bellbrook Farm, Oakford, Tiverton, Devon, EX16 9EX, 01398 351292, Water: 6 lakes total 5.5 acres. Species: Rainbow Trout, Wild Brown Trout. Charges: Normal lakes from £5.50 + pay by weight (evening) to specimen lakes £37 per day (4 fish), Other tickets available. Season: Open all year 8.00am to 9.00pm / dusk (No later than 9.00pm). Methods: Fly only.

TOTNES

Newhouse Fishery
Contact: Adrian Cook, Newhouse Farm,

Moreleigh, Totnes, Devon 01548 821426, Water: 4 Acre lake. Species: Rainbow Trout, Brown Trout. Permits: At above. Charges: 5 Fish £20, 4 Fish £17, 3 Fish £14, 2 Fish £11. Season: Open all year. Methods: Fly only, Barbed hooks.

TRURO

Gwarnick Mill Fishery
Contact: Sue Dawkins, Gwarnick Mill, St Allen, Truro, Cornwall, TR4 9QU, 01872 540487, Water: 1.5 Acre spring and river fed lake. Species: Rainbow Trout. Charges: 4 Fish £16, 3 Fish £13.50, 2 Fish £10. , Season: Open all year. Methods: Barbless Hook preferred.

Ventontrissick Trout Farm
Contact: Gerald Wright, St Allen, Truro, Cornwall TR4 9DG, 01872 540497, Water: 1/2 Acre. Species: Rainbow Trout 1.25lb - 10lb. Charges: £4.50 per day rod ticket, £1.50 per lb fish killed, First two fish to be killed, thereafter release optional. Season: 8.00am till 1hr after sunset 10 p.m. Methods: Fly only, Barbless if releasing.

WINKLEIGH

Stafford Moor Fishery
Contact: Mr Joynson, Dolton, Winkleigh, N.Devon 01805 804360, Water: 4 lakes. Species: Rainbow + Brown trout. Charges: 5 fish day £18, 4 fish day £15, 3 fish day £13, 2 fish 5 hour / eve £8, extra fish £4.50 per fish. Free fishing Darch lake, fish 4.5lb + at £8 each fish. Magpie lake fish from 1 - 1.25lb at £2.50 each. No catch & release. Season: Open all year. Methods: Fly only.

STILLWATER COARSE

BARNSTAPLE

Riverton House & Lakes
Contact: Hugh & Rosemary Smith, Swimbridge, Barnstaple, Devon EX32 0QX, 01271 830009, Water: Two x 2 acre lakes. Species: Carp Bream, Roach, Rudd, Tench, Perch, Gudgeon. Permits: Agent for Environment Agency rod licences. Charges: on application. Season: Open all year. Methods: Barbless hooks, No bolt rigs.

Little Comfort Farm
Contact: Mr Rolf Alvsaker, Braunton, N. Devon EX33 2NJ 01271 812414, Water: 1 acre approx. Species: Carp, Rudd, Roach, Tench, Orfe. Charges: £5 all day, £4 half day, £3 evening, Methods: Common sense

BEAWORTHY

Legge Farm Coarse Fishery
Contact: Simon Hockaday, Church Road, Highampton, Beaworthy, Devon, EX21 5LF, 01409 231464, Water: 1.25 Acre lake & two other ponds. Species: Carp, Tench, Perch, Roach, Rudd, Crucians, Grass Carp. Permits: On site. Charges: Adults £4.50, O.A.Ps &

Juniors £3 & evenings after 4pm. Season: All year 7am - Dusk. Night fishing by prior arrangement. Methods: Barbless hooks, Landing nets, No radios and keepnets.

Anglers Eldorado
Contact: Zyg or Bailiff Don Parsons, The Gables, Winsford, Halwill, Beaworthy, Devon, EX21 5XT, 01409 221559, Water: Four lakes from 1 acre to 4 acres. Species: Carp, Grass Carp, Wels Catfish, Golden Tench, Golden Orfe, Blue orfe, Golden Rudd, Koi. Permits: Also from Halwill Newsagents. Charges: £4 per day per rod, £3 Juniors & O.A.Ps. Season: All year, 8a.m. to dusk or 9p.m. (Which ever is earlier). Methods: Barbless hooks, No keep nets or sacks.

Anglers Shangrila
Contact: Mr Zyg Gregorek, The Gables, Winsford, Halwill, Beaworthy, . Devon, EX21 5XT 01409 221559, Water: Three match only lakes of 40 pegs, 100 pegs, 100 pegs. Species: Carp, Golden Tench, Golden Orfe. Permits: From Zyg only. Charges: You book the whole lake charges depend on how many. Season: All year. Methods: Barbless hooks.

BIDEFORD

Fosfelle Country House Hotel
Hartland, Bideford, Devon 01237 441273, Water: 1/2 acre pond approx. Species: Carp, Tench, Roach, Rudd, Charges: £5 per day. Season: Open all year. Methods: Displayed on site.

Hartland Forest
Woolsery, Bideford, Devon EX39 5RA, 01237 431442, Water: 3 acre lakes. Species: Carp. Charges: £5 per day. Season: No night fishing. Methods: No keep nets, No barbs. Clifford Farm Estate, Woolfardisworthy, Nr Bideford, North Devon EX39 5RB 01237 431319, Water: Small well established lake, Species, Carp & Tench, Charges: On application.

BODMIN

Lakeview Country Club
Contact: Paul Pearce, Old Coach Road, Lanivet, Bodmin, Cornwall, PL30 5JJ, 01208 831079, Water: 2 lakes, 4 acres in total. Species: 13 in total inc. Carp, Tench, Bream & Roach. Permits: On site Tackle Shop & Main Reception. Charges: £4 per day Adult, £2.50 Junior, O.A.P. Disabled. Methods: No boilies or night fishing.

BUDE

Bude Canal Angling Association
Contact: Mr Dick Turner, 2 Pathfields, Bude, Cornwall EX23 8DW, 01288 353162, Water: Bude Canal (1 1/4 Miles). Species: Mirror, Common, Crucian Carp, Bream, Tench, Roach, Rudd, Perch, Eels, Gudgeon, Dace. Permits: On the bank. Charges: Seniors day £3, Seniors Week £15, Juniors & O.A.Ps day £1.50, Juniors & O.A.Ps week £10. Season: Closed season April 1st May 31st inc. Methods: Micro barb or barbless hooks only, Strictly one rod only, No camping or any equipment deemed to be associated with camping.

CREDITON

Salmon Hutch Coarse Fishery
Contact: Mr Mortimer, Uton, Crediton 01363 772749, Water: 3 x 1 acre lakes. Species: Mirror and Common Carp, Rudd, Tench. Permits: On Site. Charges: Day fishing 7am to 10pm, from £4 for Adults. Night fishing 9pm to 7am, from £4 (prior booking required) Evening fishing from £2.50. Season: All Year. Methods: Barbless hooks, no long shank bent hooks, no permanently fixed lead rigs. Minimum 8lb line for carp, 4lb for general fishing. No carp in keep nets. Full rules from the fishery.

Creedy Lakes
Contact: Sandra Turner, Longbarn, Crediton, Devon EX17 4AB, 01363 772684, Water: 4.5 acre & 1/2 acre spring fed lakes, Species: Common, Mirror & Koi Carp plus Tench, Charges: £5 day ticket, £2.50 evening ticket. Season: March through to end December, Methods: Barbless Hooks, Minimum line 8lbs, No keepnets or nut baits.

CULLOMPTON

Millhayes Fishery
Contact: Mr Tony Howe, Millhayes, Kentisbeare, Cullompton, Devon, EX15 2AF, 01884 266412, Water: 2 Acre spring fed lake, plus new 1 1/2 acre Tench lake opening 1998. Species: Carp, Tench, Roach, Rudd. Charges: £4 Adults, £2.50 Under 16, £3 Evenings. Season: 1st March - 31st December. Methods: Barbless hooks only, No boilies, No night fishing, No carp in nets, Nets to be dipped, No dogs.

Upton Lakes
Contact: Chris Down, Lower Upton, Cullompton, Devon EX15 1RA, 01884 33097, Water: 1 1/2 acres of water. Species: Carp, Bream, Tench, Perch, Roach & Rudd. Season: Dawn until dusk. No night fishing. Methods: Barbless hooks, No boilies, No peanuts.

Pound Pond Farm
Contact: Mr A.R.Davey, Butterleigh, Cullompton, Devon 01884 855208, Water: Small spring fed pond. Species: Mirror, Common Carp, Roach, Tench, Perch, Rudd. Charges: £3 per rod per day, £1.50 children. Season: All year. Methods: Barbless hooks only. No Boilies.

Billingsmoor Farm
Contact: Mr & Mrs Berry, Butterleigh, Cullompton, Devon 01884 855248, Water: 4 Lakes totalling approx 3 acres + 3 lakes in 1 acre. Species: 1 Carp lake, Mixed coarse fishing ponds. Charges: From £3.50 - £5.50 per day, Evening and season tickets available. Season: Open all year. Methods: Barbless hooks only.

DAWLISH

Ashcombe Lakes
Contact: Ashcombe Training & Activities Ltd, Ashcombe, Near Dawlish, South Devon 01626 866766, Water: 3 Lakes approx 3 acres. Species: Carp, Tench, Roach. Charges: Adults £4, Juniors £3.50, £2 tickets available. Season: Open all Year. Methods: Barbless Hooks, No large Carp to be kept in keep nets.

EXETER

Exeter & Dist. Angling Assoc.
Contact: Barry Lucas, Mayfield, Gorwyn Lane, Cheriton Bishop, Exeter. 01647 24566 Water: 26 miles of River, Canal, Lakes, Ponds in Exeter area. Species: Bream, Carp, Roach, Rudd, Chub, Pike, Perch. Permits: Exeter Angling Centre, Smythen Street (Off market street). Bridge Cafe, Countess Weir. Braileys Field Sports, Market Street. County Sports, Station Road, Cullompton. Exmouth Tackle & Sport, The Strand, Exmouth. Drum Sports, Courtenay Street, Newton Abbot. Exe Valley Angling, West Exe South, Tiverton. Charges: £20 per adult, £6 for Juniors 12 & over. Season: Various - details from association. Methods: No live or deadbait coarse fish.

Bussells
Contact: Mr David Down, Bussells, Huxham, Stoke Cannon, Exeter, EX5 4EN, 01392 860612, Water: 3 Lakes. Species: Carp, Tench, Bream, Roach. Permits: Collected on site. Charges: £5 for two rods. Season: All year. Methods: Barbless Hooks, No Boilies.

South View Farm
Contact: Mr R.K.Gorton, South View Farm, Shillingford Saint George, Exeter EX2 9UP, 01392 832278, Water: 3 Lakes totalling 3 acres. Species: Mirror, Common & Ghost Carp, Roach, Rudd, Perch, Bream, Green & Gold Tench. Permits: Tickets on the bank. Charges: £5 for two rods, Juniors (under 16) £4 (must be accompanied). , Season: Open all year round. Methods: Barbless hooks, No boilies, No keep nets.

Upham Farm Ponds
Contact: S.J.Willcocks, Upham Farm, Farringdon, Exeter EX5 2HZ, 01395 232247, Water: 6 Well stocked ponds. Species: Carp, Tench. Permits: Day tickets on bank. Charges: £4 per day (concessions for O.A.P.'s, Junior). Methods: Barbless hooks, No keep nets.

Hogsbrook Lakes
Contact: Desmond & Maureen Pearson, Russett Cottage, Greendale Barton, Woodbury Salterton, Exeter, EX5 1EW, 01395 233340, Water: 1 x 1 1/2 acre, 1 x 2 acre lake. , Species: Bream, Carp, Roach, Rudd, Golden Rudd, Carp. Permits: At lakeside from bailiff, Night fishing by prior arrangement. Charges: £3 per day (One Rod) £1 extra per rod. Night £5.50 (One Rod) £1 extra per rod. Season: Open all year. Methods: Barbless hooks, Keep nets by arrangement, No Carp in nets or sacks, All Carp anglers must have unhooking mats.

Home Farm Fishery
Contact: Mr F Williams, Home Farm, Mamhead, Kenton, Exeter, Devon 01626 866259, Species: Carp, Roach, Tench, Rudd. Charges: £4 per day one rod, £4.50 two rods, weekly ticket £20 max two rods, concessions for children. Season: Open all year.

HAYLE

Sharkey's Pit
Contact: Dave Burn, Strawberry Lane, Joppa, Hayle, Cornwall 01736 753386, Water: 2 lakes approx 2 1/2 acres. Species: Common, Crucian, Mirror + Ghost Carp, Tench, Golden Orfe, Roach, Rudd, Gudgeon + Eels. Season: Open all year.

HELSTON

Middle Boswin Farm
Contact: Jonno, Middle Boswin Farm, Porkellis, Helston, Cornwall 01209 860420, Water: 1 Acre lake. Species: Carp, Roach, Rudd, Bream, Tench. Permits: Day tickets available at farm. Charges: Adult £4, concessions £3, Second rod £1 extra. Season: Winter; Dawn to Dusk, Summer 7a.m. - 9 p.m. Methods: Barbless hooks to size 8, No fixed ledgers, No cereal groundbait, hemp or nuts, No keep nets or Carp sacks.

HOLSWORTHY

Woodacott Arms
Contact: Len Sanders, Woodacott Cross, Thornbury, Holsworthy, Devon, EX22 7BT, 01409 261358, Water: 2 Lakes, 1 1/4 Acre, 1 Acre. Species: Carp, Tench, Bream, Rudd, Roach. Charges: Adults; Day Tickets 2 Rods £5, Juniors; 2 Rods £3. Methods: Barbless Hooks, No Keep Nets, No Boilies or Peanuts.

Exmoor Farm
Contact: Mr A R Mills, Week St. Mary, Holsworthy, Devon EX22 6UX, 01566 781366, Species: Tench, Golden Orfe, Rudd, Crucian, Common & Mirror Carp. Charges: £3 Per rod per day, cheaper rates after 5pm. Methods: No boilies or hemp.

Eastcott Farm & Lodges
Contact: David Whitmill, Eastcott Farm, North Tamerton, Nr Holsworthy, Devon, EX22 6SB, 01409 271172, Water: 2 Lakes totalling approx 2 acres. Species: Carp & Rudd, Charges: Day ticket £3.50, Under 16 & OAP £2.00, Residents free. Season: Open all year. Methods: Barbless hooks, No Keep Nets.

Simpson Valley Fishery
Simpson Farm, Holsworthy, Devon EX22 6JW, 01409 253593, Water: 4 lakes, New lake opening 1999. Species: Carp, Tench, Roach, Rudd, Gudgeon. Charges: £4 per day - 2 rods, £2 Juniors and O.A.P.'s.

Clawford Vineyard
Clawton, Devon EX22 6PN, 01409 254177, Water: 10 lakes. Species: Common, Mirror, Crucian, Ghost & Grass Carp, Tench, Roach, Rudd, Orfe, Barbel, Golden Tench, Blue Tench, Golden/Pink Orfe, Green Rudd, Gold Carp, Goldfish, Catfish, Ide, Chub. Charges: On application, Season: Open all year, Methods: No live or deadbait. No particles or nuts except hemp or sweetcorn. Barbless hooks only. No carp whatsoever in keepnets. Full rules at the fishery.

HONITON

Fish Ponds House
Contact: Rick Cattle, Fishponds House, Dunkeswell, Honiton EX14 OSH, 01404 891358, Water: 2 Lakes each over 1 acre. Species: Carp, Rudd, Roach and Tench. Charges: £4.00 per day, Children under 11yrs £2.00 per day, Methods: Barbless hooks, No boilies, No keep nets.

Milton Farm Ponds
Contact: Brian Cook, Milton Farm,

Payhembury, Honiton, Devon, EX14 0HE, 01404 850236, Water: 5 Lakes approx 2 acres. Species: Carp Tench, Roach, Bream. Permits: Collected on bank. Charges: £3 per person per day - no charge for extra rods, £2 children 14 + under. Season: Open all year round. Methods: No boilies, groundbait permitted.

ILFRACOMBE
Mill Park Coarse Fishing Lake
Contact: Brian & Mary Malin, Mill Park, Mill Lane, Berrynarbor, Ilfracombe, North Devon, EX34 9SH, 01271 882647, Water: 1 1/2 acre lake between Ilfracombe and Combe Martin. Species: Bream, Carp, Perch, Roach, Rudd, Tench, Golden Orfe, Golden Tench, Crucian Carp. Charges: £3.50 Adult, £2 Junior, £5 Father & Son. Reduced rates for residents of touring and camping site. Season: Lake open all year. Methods: Barbless hooks, dip all nets.

KINGSBRIDGE
Coombe Water Fisheries
Contact: J.W. Robinson, Coombe Farm, Kingsbridge, Devon TQ7 4AB, 01548 852038, Water: 3 Lakes. Species: Carp, Bream, Tench, Roach. Permits: No E.A. licence required. Lakes are covered by general E.A. licence. Charges: £4 day ticket, £2 Under 16. Season: All year dawn to dusk. Methods: Barbless hooks, No ground bait, no Carp over 1lb in keep nets.
Bickerton Farm Fishery
Contact: Mr Graham Tolchard, Bickerton Farm, Hallsands, Kingsbridge 01548 511220, Water: 1/3 acre & 3/4 acre ponds. Species: Carp, Roach, Rudd, Perch, Tench, Bream. Charges: £2.50 Under 16's, £3.50 per rod, Two rods £4 & £6. Methods: Barbless hooks, No keep nets unless fishing match.
Slapton Ley National Nature Reserve
Contact: Chris Riley, Slapton Ley Field Centre, Slapton, Kingsbridge, Devon TQ7 2QP, 01548 580685, Water: 180 acre Freshwater Lagoon, Species: Pike, Perch, Roach, Rudd, Permits: Hired rowing boats only, Charges: Dependent on number in boat e.g. £15 for 2 anglers, Season: No close season, Methods: No bank fishing.
Valley Springs
Contact: J Bishop, Sherford, Nr Kingsbridge, Devon 01548 531574, Water: 2 Lakes totalling approx 3 acres, Trout & Coarse. Species: Rainbow & Brown Trout. Charges: £7 per visit + £2 per lb. , Season: Open all year. Methods: Barbless hooks, Traditional fly fishing methods only.

LAUNCESTON
St. Leonards Coarse Fishing Lake
Contact: Andy Reeve, St. Leonards Equitation Centre, Polson, Launceston 01566 775543, Water: 2 Acre lake. Species: Carp, Rudd, Bream, Perch, Tench. Charges: £3.50 per rod per day. Season: Open all year. Methods: Barbless hooks, No ground bait.
Dutson Water
Contact: Mr or Mrs E.J.Broad Lower Dutson Farm, Launceston, Cornwall 01566 772607,

Water: 3/4 acre lake. Species: Carp, Tench, Bream, Rudd etc. Permits: Available on farm and Homeleigh Garden Centre, Dutson. Tel: 01566 773147. Charges: On application. Season: Open all year.
Stowford Grange Fisheries
Contact: Mr M.R. Sherring & Mr K.H. Ashworthy, Pets on Parade, 8 Whitehart Arcade, Launceston. Water: 2.5 acre, 1 acre and 1.25 acre Lakes. Species: Roach, Rudd, Carp, Bream, Tench, Perch, Gudgeon, Golden Tench. Permits: Day: Pets on Parade 01566 777230 & Bude Angling Supplies 01288 353306. Evenings Tel: 01752 362824 or 01566 773963, Charges: Adult £4.50 Junior £2.50. Methods: Barbless or Whisker Barbs. No boilies in bottom lake. No nuts. No carp in nets.
Elmfield Farm Coarse Fishery
Contact: Mr J Elmer, Elmfield Farm, Canworthy Water, Launceston, Cornwall 01566 781243, Water: 2 Lakes 2 acres & 1.25, Species: Carp to 20lb, Tench, Roach, Perch, Bream, Orfe & Koi, Charges: £4 - 2 Rods, £3 Children/OAP's, Season: Open all year, Methods: No keep nets, ground bait in feeders only, barbless hooks, no boilies.
Tredidon Lakes
Contact: Mr Jones, Tredidon Barton, St. Thomas, Launceston, Cornwall 01566 86463, Water: 2 lakes, Species: Common, Mirror, Crucian & Ghost Carp, Tench, Roach, Bream & Rudd. Charges: Day Tickets from £3 for 2 rods. Season: Open all year.

LOOE
Shillamill Lakes
Contact: Rick, Lanreath, Looe, Cornwall PL13 2PE, 01503 220886, Water: 3 Lakes totalling approx 5 acres. Species: Main specimen lake; Common + mirror + leather carp. Second; Common, mirror + ghost, roach, tench, crucians, perch. Third; Common + mirror, golden rudd, golden orfe, perch, tench + roach + crucian. Charges: £5 per day, £3.50 Juniors/Concession. Season: Open all year dawn till dusk. Methods: Totally barbless, boilies only on top lake, no nuts peas or beans.

NEWQUAY
White Acres Country Park
Contact: White Cross, Newquay, Cornwall 01726 860220, Water: 5 Lakes totalling approx 13 acres. Species: Wide range of almost all species. Permits: Reception. Charges: £10 per day specimen lake, £6 per day coarse lakes (Non residents). Season: April 2nd - October 3rd. Methods: 'The Method' is banned, Barbless hooks preferred, Some keepnet restrictions, No peas, nuts, or beans.
Oakside Fishery
Contact: Brian & Sandra Hiscock, 89 Pydar Close, Newquay, Cornwall TR7 3BT, 01637 871275, Water: 3 Acre Lake. Species: Mixed. Permits: Pay Kiosk, or from bailiff. Charges: Adult £3.50 (Two Rods), Junior, O.A.P's, Disabled £2.50 (Two Rods), Season: All year round. Methods: Barbless hooks, No tiger

nuts or peanuts and no Carp in keep nets.
Trebellan Park
Contact: Kevin Jago, Trebellan Park, Cubert, Newquay, Cornwall, TR8 5PY, 01637 830522, Water: 3 Lakes totalling 2.5 acres. Species: Carp, Roach, Rudd, Tench. Charges: Day tickets £3.50 1 rod, £5 two rods. Season: No close season, 7 a.m. to dusk. Methods: Barbless hooks only, No keep nets, No ground bait, no boilies.
Gwinear Pools
Contact: Simon & Jo Waterhouse, Gwinear Farm, Cubert, Newquay, Cornwall, TR8 5JX, 01637 830165, Water: 3 acre mixed lake, 60 peg match lake, Species: Carp, Roach, Bream, Perch, Rudd, Tench, Charges: Day Tickets from farm: £4 adult. £2.50 OAP's & Juniors. Evening £2.50 & £1.50, Season: No Close season, Methods: Barbless hooks. No keep nets.

NORTH TAWTON
Spires Lakes
Contact: Barry Ware, Riverside, Fore Street, North Tawton 01837 82499, Water: Two lakes, 2 acres and 1 acre. Species: Carp, Tench, Roach, Rudd, Bream, Perch, Orfe. Permits: On site kiosk, self service. Charges: £4.50 Day ticket, £3 Evening, £2.50 Junior & O.A.Ps. Methods: Barbless hooks, No boilies, No tiger or peanuts.

OKEHAMPTON
Alder Farm Lake
Contact: Mr Bob Westlake, Alder Farm, Lewdown, Okehampton, Devon 01566 783397, Water: 4 Acre Lake. Species: Perch, Roach, Carp, Tench, Bream, Plus natural stock of Trout. Charges: £3 Per rod per day. Season: No closed season / Night fishing allowed. Methods: No restrictions.

PAIGNTON
New Barn Angling Centre
Contact: Mr & Mrs R.W. Coleman, Newbarn Farm, Totnes Road, Paignton, Devon, TQ4 7PT, 01803 553602, Water: 1 Acre lake, 3 x 1/4 Acre pools, plus trout pools. Species: Carp, Tench, Roach, Bream, Perch. Charges: £5 per person per day, £3 Under 14's. Season: No closed season. Methods: No barbed hooks, keep nets or ground bait.
Town Parks Coarse Fishing Centre
Contact: Mr Paul Gammin, Town Park Farm, Totnes Road, Paignton 01803 523133, Water: 2 acre lake. Species: Common, Crucian, Mirror Carp, Bream, Tench, Roach, Perch, Rudd. Charges: Full day £5, 5 hours £4, Summer evening £3, Night fishing £7. Season: All year, Dawn - Dusk. Night fishing by appointment. Methods: Barbless hooks, Ground bait, Boilies etc in moderation.

PENZANCE
Choone Farm Fishery
Contact: Mr VB Care, Choone Farm, St Buryan, Penzance, Cornwall 01736 810220, Water: 2 lakes, Species: Carp, Tench, Perch, Rudd, Charges: 1 rod - £3.50 person, 2 rods

117

- £4.50, Season: Please telephone before travelling, Methods: Barbless hooks only, No carp in keep nets

Marazion Angling Club

Contact: Mr Bill Knott, Little Bosvenning, Newbridge, Penzance. 01736 365638. Water: Wheal Grey 3.5 acre lake, St Erth 3 acre lake, Bills Pool 2.5 acre lake. Species: All mixed fisheries. Charges: Local membership £30 per year, Out of county £20 per year. Season: Open all year Methods: Any.

Tindeen Fishery

Contact: J Laity, Bostrase, Millpool, Goldsithney, Penzance, TR20 9JG, 01736 763486, Water: 3 Lakes approx 1 acre each. Species: Carp, Roach, Rudd, Gudgeon, Perch, Trout. Charges: Adults £3, Juniors under 14 £2, Extra rod £1 each. Season: All year, Night fishing by arrangement. Methods: Barbless hooks to be used.

PERRANPORTH

Bolingey Lakes

Contact: Mike or Jan, Penwartha Road, Bolingey, Nr Perranporth, Cornwall 01872 572388, Water: 1 Lake approx 4 acres. Species: All types Carp, Roach, Rudd, Perch, Tench, Koi. Permits: On site. Charges: £5 per day per person, Disabled, O.A.P.'s Juniors (under 12) £3.50. Season: Open all year. Methods: No Trout pellets, Ground bait, Barbless hooks only, No keep nets. Full rules displayed on lodge.

ST. AUSTELL

Roche (St Austell) Angling Club

Contact: Mr Colin Stephens - Secretary, 150 Killyvarder Way, St Austell. 01726 67704. Water: 6 fresh water lakes in St Austell area. Species: Roach, Perch, Rudd, Tench, Eels, Carp, Pike & Bream. Permits: Fishing restricted to Members and their guests only. Membership applications available at local Angling Shops. Charges: Full Annual membership £30, concessionary £10 plus initial joining fee. Membership to game and sea section only at reduced rates. Season: Open all year Methods: As specified in club byelaws.

SALTASH

Bush Lakes

Contact: J Renfree, Bush Farm, Saltash, Cornwall PL12 6QY, 01752 842148, Water: 4 Lakes from 1/2 - 1 Acre. Species: Carp, Tench, Rudd, Roach, Bream. Charges: £4.50 per person, two rods max. Season: Open all year. Methods: Barbless hooks, Landing Mat.

Bake Fishing Lakes

Contact: Chris Bond, Trerule Farm, Trerule Foot, Saltash, Cornwall 01503 240304, Water: 5 Lakes adding up to 14+ acres, coarse and trout. Species: Mirror, Common, Ghost, Crucian Carp, Tench, Bream, Roach, Rudd. Permits: Clives Tackle & Bait (Plymouth). Charges: £5 per day, Season: Autumn / Winter 8am - Dusk, Spring / Summer 7am - Dusk. Methods: Barbless hooks, No nuts or trout pellets.

SEATON

Wiscombe Park Fishery

Contact: Mike Raynor, Wiscombe Park Fishery, Colyton, Devon EX13 6JE, 01404 871474, Water: Half acre lake. Species: Carp, Tench, Bream. Permits: Self-service (No booking). Charges: £3.50 per day, Reduced rates for O.A.Ps & Children. Children (under 15) free if accompanied by permit holding adult. Season: All year. Methods: Single rod.

SOUTH BRENT

Little Allers Coarse Fishery

Contact: M & J Wakeham, Little Allers Farm, Avonwick, South Brent, Devon 01364 72563, Water: 2 Acre lake. Species: Carp, Bream, Tench, Roach, Rudd. Permits: On the bank. Charges: £4 per day adults, £2.50 under 16, £2.50 evening ticket after 5 p.m. Season: Open all year dawn to dusk. Methods: Barbless hooks only, No carp in keep nets, No boilies.

SOUTH MOLTON

Oaktree Fishery

Contact: George Andrews, East Anstey, Yeo Mill, South Molton, Devon, EX36 3PU, 01398 341568, Water: Three x 2 acre lakes. Species: Carp, Tench, Bream, Roach, Perch, Koi Carp, Catfish. Permits: On site only. Charges: Day tickets: Adults from £4, Specimen lake £5, Juniors from £3, Specimen lake £4, Eve tickets: Adult £3, Specimen lake £4, Junior £2.50 Specimen lake £3. Season: Open all year 24hrs.

ST COLUMB

Meadowside Fishery

Contact: Lee Evans, Meadowside Farm, Winnards Perch, St. Columb, Cornwall, TR9 6DH, 01637 880544, Water: 2 1/2 acre Carp only lake, plus 2 acre mixed coarse fishery. Species: Carp, Roach, Perch, Rudd, Tench, Bream. Charges: £3.50 & £2.50 concessions. Season: No close season, Dawn to dusk. Methods: Barbless hooks.

Retallack Waters

Contact: Winnards Perch, Nr St Columb Major, Cornwall 01637 880974, Water: 6.5 acre main lake, seperate match canal. Species: Common, Mirror and Ghost Carp, Pike, Bream, Tench, Roach and Rudd. Methods: Barbless hooks only.

TAUNTON

Lovelynch Fisheries

Contact: Mrs W.B. Loram, Lovelynch Farm, Milverton, Taunton TA4 1NR, 01823 400268, Water: 3 acre lake on farm. Species: Mainly Carp. Charges: £4 Adults, £2.50 Children. Season: All year, Dawn - Dusk. Methods: No boilies, barbless hooks, No night fishing.

TAVISTOCK

Milemead Fisheries

Contact: Mr Harry Dickens, Mill Hill, Tavistock, Devon PL19 8NP, 01822 610888, Water: 2 Lakes of 2 Acres each. Species: Carp, Tench,

Bream, Roach, Rudd. Charges: Adult £5, Concession £4 Evening tickets available. Season: All year, 7 a.m. to Dusk. Methods: Barbless Hooks, All nets to be dipped prior to fishing, Please read the rule boards.

TIVERTON

Devonshire Centre

Contact: Mr Shields, Bickleigh Mill, Bickleigh, Nr Tiverton, Devon, EX16 8RG, 01884 855419, Water: Bickleigh Mill fishing ponds. Species: Rainbow Trout with occasional Rudd, Roach, Tench. Permits: Only as above. Charges: £2.50 To include entry to Mill + Tea or Coffee (One child per adult admitted free). Season: Easter then Whitsun to end of September. Methods: Rod supplied.

Coombe Farm Fishponds

Contact: Mrs Curtis, Coombe Farm, Cadleigh, Tiverton, Devon 01884 855337, Water: 3 lakes totalling 1/2 acre. Species: Carp, Roach, Tench, Bream. Charges: £3 per day. Season: Open all year. Methods: No boilies.

Tiverton & District Angling Club

Contact: John Smallwood, Exe Valley Angling, 19 Westexe South, Tiverton. Water: 11.5 Miles on Grand Western Canal, 1.25 Acre mixed fishery lake at Exebridge. Species: Canal; Carp, Bream, Tench, Roach, Perch, Pike, Eels. Lakeside; Carp, Bream, Roach, Tench, Eels, Crucian Carp. Permits: Canal; Carp, Bream, Tench, Roach, Perch, Pike, Eels. Lakeside; Carp, Bream, Roach, Tench, Eels, Crucian Carp. Charges: Senior; Day £4, Annual £18. Conc: Day £2.50, Annual £8. Season: Canal; Closed March 1st - May 31st inc, except 2 seperate sections (Ring for details). Lakeside; Open all year, Weekends full members only, Maximum five day permits per day. Methods: Canal Methods; Any. Restrictions; Fish from permanent pegs, No night fishing, No cars on bank, No digging of banks or excessive clearance of vegatation. Lakeside Methods; Any. Restrictions; No night fishing, No boilies, Trout pellets or nuts, One rod only, Fishing from permanent pegs, No dogs, Nets to be dipped. Ring Exe Valley Angling for full details.

Westpitt Farm Fishery

Contact: Mr Rodney Crocker, Uplowman, Nr. Tiverton, Devon EX16 7PU, 01884 820296, Water: 3 Lakes up to 1.25 acres, Species: Common & Mirror Carp, Bream, Tench, Roach, Rudd,Crucians, Golden tench, Chub, Golden Orfe. Permits: Self service day tickets £3.50 per day (Correct money please), Season: All year. No closed season. Methods: No Boilies, Barbless Hooks.

TORPOINT

Millbrook

Contact: Mark Blake, Treganhawke Farmhouse, Millbrook, Torpoint, Cornwall, PL10 1JH, 01752 823210, Water: 1 Acre water in sheltered, wooded valley. Species: Perch, Tench, Carp, Crucians, Roach, Rudd, Bream. Permits: Self service at water in old phone box, correct money needed. Charges: £5 per day, £3 after 5 p.m. evening. Season: Open all year. Methods: Barbless hooks, Landing net.

TORRINGTON

Bakers Farm
Contact: Mr & Mrs Ridd, Bakers Farm, Moortown, Torrington, Devon, EX38 7ES, 01805 623260, Water: 1 Acre lake, Species: Mirror & Common Carp, Tench, Roach & Rudd, Charges: £3 per rod per day, Methods: Barbless Hooks, No large carp in keep nets.

TRURO

Mellonwatts Mill Coarse Fishery
Pensagillas Farm, Grampound, Truro, Cornwall 01872 530232, Water: 2 Acre lake. Species: Common & Mirror Carp, Roach, Tench, Golden Rudd. Charges: Day ticket £5, Evening £3. Season: Open all year.

Rosewater Lake
Contact: Mike & Andy Waters Nr Perranporth, Cornwall 01872 573992, Water: 1.5 Acre private lake. Species: Carp, Tench, Roach, Rudd, Crucians, Perch, Bream. Charges: Day ticket £4, Under 16 / O.A.Ps £2, Evening ticket £2. Season: Open all year. Methods: Barbless hooks only.

Threemilestone Angling Club
Contact: Mrs T Bailey, 9 Sampson Way, Threemilestone, Truro. 01872 272578. Water: 2 Pools. Species: Carp, Tench, Roach, Rudd, Bream, Perch, Goldfish. Permits: At lakeside. Charges: Seniors £3, Juniors £2. Season: All season, No night fishing. Methods: Barbless hooks only, No Peanuts etc.

YELVERTON

Coombe Fisheries
Contact: Mr Stephen Horn Yelverton, Nr Plymouth, Devon 01822 616624, Water: 2 x 1 Acre lakes. Species: Coarse fish. Permits: Local Post Office. Charges: £4 per day. Season: No close season, Dawn to dusk. Methods: Barbless hooks.

NORTH WESSEX
River Fishing

THE BRISTOL AVON
The River Avon flows from its sources near Sherston and Tetbury to its confluence with the Severn at Avonmouth some 117 kilometres and is fed by many tributaries on its way. The headwaters of the River Avon, the Tetbury and Sherston branches join at Malmesbury. Both are important trout streams where fishing is strictly preserved and there is little opportunity for the visiting angler to fish these waters

Malmesbury to Chippenham
Coarse fisheries predominate in this section, although trout are stocked by fishing associations in some areas. Arguably one of the best fisheries in the country, this section

contains a wide range of specimen fish. Local records include: roach 3lb 2oz, perch 3lb 3oz, tench 8lb 5 1/2oz, bream 8lb 8oz, dace 1lb 2oz, chub 7lb 10oz, carp 20lb 8 1/4oz and pike 33lb 3oz. Also many barbel to 12lb have been reported.

Chippenham to Bath
Upstream from Staverton to Chippenham the Avon continues to be an important coarse fishery, both for the pleasure angler and match fisherman. The river flows through a broad flood plain and provides a pastoral setting. In the faster flowing sections chub, roach, dace and barbel can be caught in good numbers. This year saw the local barbel record bettered with a fish of 15lb 9 1/2oz, also a bream of nearly 10lb was reported.

Bath to Hanham
Between Hanham and Bath much of this length retains a rural character and is an important coarse fishery used by pleasure and match anglers. The National Angling Championships have been held here. Roach, bream and chub are the main catches and, in some favoured swims, dace. Very good catches of bream are to be had with specimen fish. 'Free' fishing is available through Bath from the towpath side between Newbridge and Pulteney Weir. Carp of 20lb have been reported caught downstream of Pulteney and Keynsham Weirs.

Hanham to Avonmouth
Between Netham Dam and Hanham Weir the river is affected by spring tides. The water has a very low saline content and this length of river provides reasonable coarse fishing. Below Netham Dam the river contains mostly estuarine species but some sea trout and salmon have been seen.

BRISTOL FROME
The Bristol Frome rises at Dodington and offers a fair standard of coarse fishing on the lower sections The upper section contains limited stocks of brown trout, roach and perch. This tributary of the River Avon is culverted beneath Bristol and discharges into the Floating Harbour.

RIVER BOYD
The River Boyd rises just south of Dodington and joins the Bristol Avon at Bitton. In the middle and lower reaches coarse fish predominate. The upper reaches above Doynton contain brown trout.

BY BROOK
The Broadmead and Burton brooks together form the By Brook which flows through Castle Combe and is joined by several smaller streams before entering the River Avon at Bathford. Brown trout predominate above the village of Box, mostly small in size but plentiful in number. At Box and below the fishery is mixed and dace to 14oz and roach of 2lb are not uncommon.

RIVER MARDEN
The River Marden is fed by springs rising from the downs above Cherhill and joins the river Avon upstream of Chippenham. Brown trout occur naturally in the upper reaches. Downstream of Calne coarse fish predominate and weights of more than 30lb are regularly caught in matches. This year saw the Marden

barbel record rise to over 10lb.

SEMINGTON BROOK
The Semington Brook is spring fed from Salisbury Plain and flows through a flat area to its confluence with the River Avon downstream of Melksham. In the upper reaches and in some of its tributaries brown trout predominate. Downstream of Bulkington coarse fish prevail with sizeable bream, chub, roach, dace and perch.

SOMERSET FROME
The Somerset Frome is the main tributary of the Bristol Avon. It drains a large catchment area which is fed from the chalk around Warminster and limestone from the eastern end of the Mendips. There are numerous weirs and mills mostly disused. The tributaries above Frome provide ideal conditions for brown trout with fishing on the River Mells. The middle and lower reaches provide excellent coarse fishing.

CAM AND WELLOW BROOKS
The Cam and Wellow Brooks, rising on the north side of the Mendip Hills, flow through what was a mining area and now provide good quality trout fishing controlled by local fishing associations.

MIDFORD BROOK
The Midford Brook runs through well wooded valleys with mostly mixed fishing on the lower reaches and trout fishing in upper reaches. The largest brown trout recorded weighed 5lb 6oz.

RIVER CHEW
The River Chew rises near Chewton Mendip and flows through the Bristol Waterworks Reservoirs at Litton and Chew Valley Lake. The river continues through Chew Magna, Stanton Drew, Publow, Woolard and Compton Dando to its confluence with the River Avon at Keynsham. A mixed fishery for most its length and is particularly good for roach, dace and grayling below Pensford.

KENNET AND AVON CANAL
There are some 58 kilometres of canal within the Bristol Avon catchment area which averages one metre in depth and thirteen metres in width. The Kennet & Avon Canal joins the River Avon at Bath with the River Kennet between Reading and Newbury. The canal was opened in 1810 to link the Severn Estuary with the Thames. The canal, now much restored, provides excellent fishing with carp to 25lb, tench to 5lb also roach, bream, perch, rudd, pike and gudgeon.

Bristol, Avon & Tributaries Angling Association
Contact: Secretary, 1 Adelaide Place, Bath BA2 6BU, 01225 462760, Water: Somerset Frome, Cam, Wellow, Midford Brooks., Species: Coarse., Charges: No day tickets, season guest ticket £92 for four visits., Season: In rules., Methods: In rules.

Bristol, Frome Angling Association
Contact: Roger Lee, 51 Welshmill Lane, Frome, Somerset BA11 3AP, 01373 461433, Water: 12 miles River Frome - 10 acre lake., Species: River: Roach, Chub, Bream. Lake: Tench, Carp, Roach, Pike., Permits: Frome Angling Centre, 11 Church Street, Frome.

Haines Angling, Christchurch Street West, Frome., Charges: £10 Senior, £5 Junior U/16, O.A.P's £1.50, Day tickets £2. Methods: No restrictions.

Bathampton Angling Association
Contact:Dave Crookes, 25 Otago Terrace, Larkhill, Bath BA1 6SX, 01225 427164, Water: 2 Acre lake at Newton Park, 3 Lakes - Total 6 acres at Hunstrete, 1 Acre lake at Woodbrough, Lydes Farm Lake. 6 Miles Kennet & Avon canal Bath to Limpley Stoke, 3 Miles River Avon Kelston to Bath, 2 Miles River Avon at Claverton, 5 Miles trout fishing on Box Brook (Fly Only). Species: Carp, Tench, Bream, Roach, Dace, Barbel, Perch, Chub.Trout. Permits: Tackle Shops in Bristol & Bath area., Charges: Adults £17.50, Lady & Gent combined £25, Juniors (Under 17) £4.50, O.A.Ps £3.50, Registered disabled £4.50. Season: All year on lakes. River season details and maps of lakes on request., Methods: Barbless hooks, No keep nets as indicated in membership card.

Bristol City Docks Angling Club
Contact: Bob Taylor 01454 773990, Water: 3 mile on Bristol Avon from Chequers Weir to Netham., Species: Skimmers, Bream, Roach, Dace, Chub, Pike, Eels., Permits: All Bristol tackle shops and Harbour Masters office., Charges: Feeder canal (between Avon + Dock) Season £10, Concessions, Juniors, O.A.P's £5, Day tickets £2.50 + £1.50 in advance, £4 + £2 on bank. River Avon free fishing., Season: April - March 31st inclusive, River - normal close season applies, Dock closed season on all year except Baltic Wharf.

Bristol, Bath & Wiltshire Amalgamated Anglers
Contact: JS Parker, 16 Lansdown View, Kingswood, Bristol BS15 4AW, 0117 9672977, Water: Approx 80 miles Coarse Fishing on Bristol Avon & Somerset Rivers & Streams. Stillwaters at Lyneham, Calne, Malmesbury, Bath and Pawlett near Bridgwater. Trout only water on Cam Brook. Too much to list here, please contact the secretary for full details., Species: All coarse species, Permits: Full Membership available from the Secretary. Veterans over 70 years may apply in writing for free full membership sending SAE to Secretary. Full members only may fish at Tockenham Resevoir, Burton Hill lake at Malmesbury & Shackells Lake. Day Tickets for all waters except Burton Hill & Tockenham are available at Tackle Shops., Methods: No night Fishing. No metal cans/ glass bottles in possesion. No fresh water fishes as live bait. Maximum 2 rods per angler. Full rules on application.

Calne Angling Association
Contact: Miss JM Knowler, 123a London Road, Calne, Wiltshire 01249 812003, Water: River Avon, River Marden and a lake., Species: Barbel, Pike, Carp, Bream, Rudd, Roach etc., Season: River: June - March, Lake: open all year, Methods: No restrictions.

Chippenham Angling Club
Contact: Mr Duffield 01249 655575, Water: 8 miles on River Avon + Carp lake at Corsham., Species: Barbel, Chub, Roach, Bream, Perch, Pike, Tench., Permits: Robs Tackle,

Chippenham - Tel: 01249 659210., Charges: Please telephone for 1998 prices., Methods: No boilies or keep nets on Carp lake.

Marlborough & District A.A.
Contact: Mr.M.Ellis, Failte, Elcot Close, Marlborough, Wilts, SN8 2BB, 01672 512922, Water: Kennet & Avon Canal (12 miles approx). Species: Roach, Perch, Pike, Tench, Bream, Carp. Charges: Full membership £23 + £5 joining fee, Junior up to 16 £5, Ladies £5, O.A.P's £5., Season: Fishing as close season, 14th March (end) - 16th June (start). Membership from 1st Jan - 31st Dec 1998., Methods: No live baiting, No bloodworm or joker.

Pewsey & District Angling Association
Contact: Don Underwood, 51 Swan Meadow, Pewsey, Wiltshire SN9 5HP, 01672 562541, Water: 4 Miles Kennet & Avon canal. Species: Roach, Tench, Carp, Bream, Perch, Pike., Permits: The Wharf, Pewsey., Charges: Day tickets Senior £3 / Junior/OAP £2., Season: June 16th - March 14th., Methods: Rod and line.

Cameley Lakes
See entry under stillwater trout, Bristol. Fishing on River Cam.,

RIVER TONE

The River Tone rises on the edge of Exmoor National Park and not far from its source it feeds into and out of Clatworthy reservoir. From here to Taunton there are some twenty miles of fast flowing trout river, though grayling, dace and roach appear near Taunton where weirs provide increased depth. Through the town and just below, chub, dace and roach predominate but at Bathpool the river becomes wider, deeper and slower. Roach, bream, carp, tench and pike are the typical species in this stretch which continues to the tidal limit at New Bridge.

Taunton Angling Association
See entry under Taunton and Bridgwater Canal. 6 miles on River Tone.,
Wellington Angling Association
Contact: Crofton Redstone, 10 Priory, Wellington, Somerset TA21 9EJ, 01823 662514, Water: Approx 1.5 mile on River Tone., Species: Brown Trout. Permits: Membership only., Charges: Joining fee £10, annual membership £9. Season: On application. Methods: No spinning.

BRIDGWATER & TAUNTON CANAL

Cut in 1827 the canal provided a good commercial waterway between the two towns. The canal has been recently restored for navigation but there is only infrequent boat traffic. The canal offers excellent coarse fishing from the towpath for roach, bream, tench, rudd, perch and pike.

Bridgwater Angling Association
Contact: Mr Jon Cotton - Secretary, 74 Stoddens Road, Burnham -on-Sea, Somerset TA8 2DB, 01278 782786, Water: 6 miles on the Bridgwater & Taunton Canal, Fishing on

the rivers Parrett & Isle, Cripps, North & South Drain, King's Sedgemoor Drain, Langacre Rhine & The Huntspill. Stillwater fishing at Combwich, Walrow, Dunwear, Screech Owl & Somerset Bridge Ponds., Species: All types of Coarse Fish, Permits: Available from Tackle outlets throughout Somerset area including Somerset Angling, 74 Bath Rd, Bridgwater, Tel: 01278 431777 & Thyers Tackle, 1a Church Street, Highbridge. Tel: 01278 786934.

Taunton Angling Association
Contact: Mr.M.Hewitson, 56 Parkfield Road, Taunton, Somerset 01823 271194, Water: 7 miles on Bridgewater & Taunton Canal, 6 miles on River Tone, West Sedgemoor Drain, Wych Lodge Lake, Walton & King Stanley Ponds, Wellington Basins., Species: Most Coarse species (excluding Barbel). Permits: Topp Tackle, 63 Station Road, Taunton, (01823) 282518. Enterprise Angling (01823) 282623. Charges: 1998 season £18. Day tickets £4 Senior, £2 Junior., Season: Closed 14th March - 16th June, Ponds open all year., Methods: Barbless hooks on stillwater. No bait restrictions.

WEST SEDGEMOOR MAIN DRAIN

This artificial channel was excavated in the 1940s on the lines of existing watercourses. Coarse fish species present include bream, roach, tench and carp.

RIVER PARRETT

The River Parrett rises in West Dorset and there is some trout fishing as far as Creedy Bridge upstream of the A303. Below this point a number of weirs and hatches result in deeper water and slower flows. The resulting coarse fishery contains a wide variety of species including roach, bream, rudd, chub, dace, carp, crucian carp and pike. Similar species are found in the lowest freshwater section at Langport where the Rivers Isle and Yeo join the Parrett to form a wide deep river which becomes tidal below Oath Sluice.

Stoke Sub Hamdon & District A.A.
Contact: Mr Derek Goad (Secretary), 2 Windsor Lane, Stoke-sub-Hamdon, Somerset, H.Q.: Stoke Working Mens Club. Water: Upper Stretches River Parrett approx 10km. Also Bearley Lake, Long Load Drain (Shared Water), Species: Carp, Tench, Roach, Rudd, Bream, Perch, Dace, Chub, Pike, Eel, Gudgeon, Ruffe. Trout Fishing also available., Permits: Stax Tackle, Montacute is the only outlet for lake tickets. Yeovil Angling Centre, Yeovil., Charges: Lake only £2.50 members. £3.50 non members. Senior £7, Concession £4. Limited Season Tickets on lake - full members only., Season: Trout 1st April - 31st October. Lake all year. Coarse 16th June - 14th March., Methods: Trout - No maggot. Lake - No boilies or nut baits. River Coarse - No restrictions.

Wessex Federation of Angling Clubs
Contact: Mr R Payne (secretary), 194 Milton Road, Weston - Super - Mare, North

120

Somerset BS22 8AE, 01934 414445, Water: 2 miles River Parrett, 1/2 mile River Isle. Species: Roach, Bream, Rudd, Chub, Carp, Tench, Perch, Gudgeon, Dace, Pike. Permits: Martin Brook, The Tackle Box, 1 Old Market Square, North Street, Langport, TA10 9RD. Charges: £2.50 per day Senior, £1.00 Junior / Disabled / O.A.P's. Season: 16th June - 14th March. Methods: Live - baiting not allowed.

RIVER ISLE

The River Isle rises near Wadeford and soon after its source is joined by a tributary from Chard Lake. Trout are found as far as Ilminster but below the town coarse fish predominate. The profile of the river is fairly natural though a number of shallow weirs provide increased depth in places. Species caught in the lower stretches include chub, dace and roach.

THE KINGS SEDGEMOOR DRAIN

The Kings Sedgemoor Drain is an artificial drainage channel dug c1790. As well as draining a large area of moor it also carries the diverted water of the River Cary and excess flood flows from the River Parrett. The KSD is a very well known coarse fishery and is used for both local and national match fishing competitions. Fish species present include roach, bream, tench, perch and pike.

RIVER AXE

The River Axe emerges from the Mendip Hills at Wookey Hole and from here to below Wookey the river is trout water. The river deepens as it crosses low lying land at the foot of the Mendips to below Bleadon and Brean Cross, the tidal limit. Fish species in the lower reaches include bream, roach, tench, dace and pike.

Weston-super-Mare A.A.
Contact: Weston Angling Centre, 25a Locking Road, Weston-super-Mare 01934 631140, Water: River Axe, River Brue, South Drain, North Drain. Species: Bream, Tench, Roach, Carp, Gudgeon, some Dace, Chub., Permits: Weston Angling Centre., Charges: Season £20, Week £10, Day £4. Season: Old River Axe, Year round., Methods: No boilies, No nuts, No dyed maggots.

RIVER KENN AND BLIND YEO

The New Blind Yeo is an artificial drainage channel which also carries some of the diverted water of the River Kenn. Both waters contain good roach with bream, rudd, carp, perch, tench and pike.

RIVER YEO

The River Yeo rises near Sherborne and between here and Yeovil the river is a coarse fishery, though tributaries such as the River Wriggle have brown trout. Below Yeovil a number of weirs produce deep water areas and the resulting fishery contains good dace together with roach, chub, bream and pike.

N. Somerset Association of Anglers
Contact: Mr R L Purchase, 28 The Tynings, Clevedon, N. Somerst BS21 7YP. 01275 878384, Water: Blind Yeo, Kenn, Congresbury Yeo, Brue, Apex Lake, Newtown Ponds & Walrow Ponds., Species: Roach, Bream, Eels, Perch, Rudd, Carp, Pike. Permits: NSAA Permits available at all local Tackle Shops, Charges: Season- Seniors £16. Juniors/OAP/ Disabled £7. Weekly £7. Day £2.50. Season: June 16th - March 14th inclusive, Methods: Barbless Hooks Apex Lake. No live/dead baits.

RIVER BRUE

The River Brue is a trout fishery from its source above Bruton to Lovington. From here to Glastonbury a number of weirs provide areas of deep water and coarse fish predominate, notably chub and roach, together with bream, dace and pike. Similar species may be found between Glastonbury and Highbridge where the river is channelled across the Somerset Levels and connected with a number of drainage channels such as the Huntspill River and North Drain.

HUNTSPILL RIVER / SOUTH DRAIN / CRIPPS RIVER / NORTH DRAIN

The Huntspill River is a man made drainage channel, excavated in the 1940s and connected to the River Brue and South Drain via the Cripps River. The North Drain was dug c1770 to drain low lying moors to the north of the River Brue. The Huntspill is a notable coarse fishery and is often the venue for national and local match fishing competitions. Catches consist primarily of bream and roach. The North and South Drain and Cripps River contain similar species and also offer good sport for the coarse angler.

STILLWATER TROUT

Bridgewater
Quantock Fishery
Contact: Sue & Neil Bruce-Miller, Quantock Fishery, Stream Farm, Broomfield, Bridgwater, Somerset, TA5 2EN, 01823 451367, Water: 2 Acre spring fed lake. Species: Rainbow Trout. Charges: Prices on application and booking advisable. Season: Open every day all year dawn to dusk. Methods: Barbless hooks only, Two fish limit - then catch + release.

Bristol
Cameley Lakes
Contact: J Harris, Hillcrest Farm, Cameley, Temple Cloud, Somerset, BS18 5AQ, 01761 452423, Water: 5 Acre lakes and fishing on the River Cam. Species: Rainbow Trout, Brown Trout. Charges: £18 incl. VAT Day ticket 4 fish, £15 incl. VAT 1/2 Day ticket 2 fish. Season: All season - 8.00 till sundown. Methods: Hooks no larger than 1 inch.

Congresbury
Silver Springs Trout Fishery
Contact: Mrs E Patch, Silver Street Lane, Congresbury, Somerset 01934 877073, Water: 2.5 Acres. Species: Rainbows. Permits: On Site. Charges: 4 Fish £18, 3 @ £15, 2 @ £12 , 2 Fish O.A.P. / U16 £11. ✝ Season: All year. Methods: Fly only.

Devizes
Mill Farm Trout Lakes
Contact: Bill Coleman, Mill Farm Trout Lakes, Worton, Devizes 01380 813138, Water: 2 Waters of 3.5 acres each. Species: Rainbow & Brown trout. Permits: Local shop. Charges: 5 Fish £24, 4 Fish £20, 3 Fish £16, 2 Fish £11. Season: All year, 7.30 - dusk. Methods: Fly fishing only.

Dulverton
Exe Valley Fishery
Contact: Hugh Maund, Exebridge, Dulverton, Somerset 01398 323328, Water: 3 Lakes fly only (2 + 1 + 3/4 acre lakes), 1 Small lake any method 1/2 acre. Species: Rainbow Trout, Brown Trout. Permits: Day Tickets. Charges: £5.50 per day + £3.50 per kilo, Evenings (after 5) April - September 3 fish limit, £3.50 plus £3.50 per kilo. Season: All year. Methods: See above.

Fairford
Milestone Fisheries
Contact: Sue or Bob Fletcher or Andy King, Milestone Fisheries, London Road, Fairford, Glos. 01285 713908, Water: 10 acre lake and 2 acre lake, Species: 10 acre lake: Brown trout, Rainbow trout 2lb - 20lb. 2 acre lake: Rainbow trout 1lb - 1.25lb. (bank fishing only). Permits: Day tickets & Season tickets. Charges: 10 acre lake: Day & season tickets. Bank (Boats & Float tube for hire) Day ticket 5 fish £30, 1/2 day 3 fish £20. 2 acre lake: bank fishing only. Catch and take only £12 for 5 fish. Season: No closed season (Return all browns). Methods: Catch & take or Catch & release on ten acre lake only. (Barbless hooks on Catch & release), Fly fishing only.

Frome
St Algars Farm Lake
Contact: Mr.A.M. Mackintosh, St Algars Farm, West Woodlands, Nr Frome, Somerset, BA11 5ER, 01985 844233, Water: 2 Acre Lake. Species: Rainbow Trout. Charges: April - May (£14, 4 Fish limit) (£8.50, 2 Fish limit) June - October (£12, 4 Fish limit) (£8.50, 2 Fish limit). Season: 1st April - 31st October, Dawn to dusk. Possible short closure end of May (advisable to telephone before journey).

Malmesbury
The Lower Moor Fishery
Contact: Geoff & Anne Raines, Lower Moor Farm, Oaksey, Malmesbury, Wilts, SN16 9TW, 01666 860232, Water: 2 Lakes, 34 acre Mallard lake, 8 acre Cottage lake. Species: Rainbow & Brown Trout. Permits: At lakeside.

Charges: 4 Fish ticket £20, 2 Fish ticket £12, Junior 2 Fish ticket £10. Season: March 21st - Jan 1st '99, 8 a.m. to dusk. Methods: Mallard lake - any type of fly fishing (nymph or dry fly), Cottage lake - nymph, dry fly or floating line.

Somerton

Viaduct Trout Fishery

Contact: Mr Robbie Winram (Manager), Viaduct Fishery, Cary Valley, Somerton, Somerset, TA11 6LU, 01458 274022, Water: 2 x 3 Acre Fly lakes plus one any method Trout Lake 1/2 Acre. Species: Rainbow Trout, Brown Trout. Permits: At Fishery Office or Pre - Payment Hut. Charges: 5-Fish £25, 4-Fish £21, 3-Fish £18, 2-Fish £14. (Sporting Ticket £6 to fish + £2 per lb. of fish). half day catch & release £9 / Full day £14. Season: Open all year. Methods: Barbless hooks, Max hook size 10, One rod at a time.

Wiveliscombe

Clatworthy Fly Fishing Club

Contact: Cofton Redstone, 10 Priory, Wellington, Somerset TA21 9EJ, 01823 662514, Water: 170 acre Clatworthy reservoir on Exmoor, Species: Rainbow and Brown Trout, Permits: On site from Lodge, Charges: Day Ticket £12 - 5 fish limit. Concessions £10 OAP's. Evening Ticket £7. Bulk day Tickets 11 for price of 10. Season £360 - 4 fish limit. Concession £260. Boats £10 per day. £6 evening. Season: Open 21 March 18 October, Methods: Fly Fishing Only.

STILLWATER COARSE

Bath

Abbey Coarse Fishery

Contact: John or Nigel Dawe - Lane, Moores Farm, Holcombe, Nr Bath, Somerset 01761 232400, Water: 3 Lakes totalling 4 acres. Species: Crucian, Mirror, Common and Ghost Carp, Tench, Rudd, Roach, Chub, Bream and Perch. Permits: On site only Tel: 01761 232400. Mobile: 0966 542297, Charges: Specimen Lake by arrangement, General lakes £4 day, Season: March 1st to November 1st, Methods: Barbless Hooks, No nut baits, No carp in keep nets.

Bathampton Angling Association

See entry under Avon. Various lakes and river fishing.

Bridgwater

Avalon Fisheries

Contact: Allan Tedder (Ted), 7 Coronation Road, Bridgwater, Somerset 01278 456429, Water: 6 acre match Coarse + 3 acre specimen lakes. Species: Carp, Tench, Bream, Roach, Rudd, Perch and Barbel. Permits: Site office and on the bank. Charges: £4 Adult, £2.50 Junior / O.A.P / Disabled. Season: No closed season - Open dawn to dusk. Methods: Barbless on specimen lake,

No floating or boilie baits on coarse lake, all nuts banned on both lakes.

Bridgwater Angling Association

See entry under Taunton and Bridgwater Canal. Various stillwaters.

Bristol

Alcove Angling Club

Contact: Mr K. Davis (Membership Secretary), 6 Ashdene Ave, Eastville, Bristol BS5 6QH, 01179 654778, Water: 4 lakes in Bristol & South Glos. Species: Carp, Bream, Roach, Tench, Rudd, Pike, Perch. Permits: As above. Charges: £27.50 Adult, £14 O.A.P / Disabled. Season: No close season. Methods: As specified in membership card, No night fishing at Alcove Lido only.

Bitterwell Lake

Contact: Mrs M Reid, The Chalet, Bitterwell Lake, Ram Hill, Coalpit Heath, Bristol, BS36 2UF, 01454 778960, Water: 2 1/2 Acres, Species: Common, Mirror, Crucian Carp, Roach, Bream, Rudd, Perch. Charges: £3.00 per rod, £1.50 O.A.P's, Reg disabled and arrivals after 4 p.m. Season: Closed for spawning 4 - 6 weeks May - June. Methods: Barbless hooks size 8 biggest, No bolt rigs, No boilies, No nuts, Hemp or groundbait.

Bristol, Bath & Wiltshire Amalgamated Anglers

See entry under Avon. Various stillwaters. Too much to list here, please contact the secretary for full details.

Paulton Lakes

Contact: Trevor Francis, Paulton, Bristol 01761 413081, Water: 2 lakes totalling 2 1/2 acres. Species: Carp, Tench, Roach, Grass Carp, Rudd, Chub. Permits: Only from Paulton Builders Merchants, Paulton and A.M. Hobbs, Midsomer Norton. Tel (01761) 413961. Season: Open all year, Dawn to dusk. Methods: Barbless hooks, No ground baiting, Unhooking mats must be used.

Tan House Farm Lake

Contact: Mr & Mrs James, Tan House Farm, Yate, Bristol BS37 7QL, 01454 228280, Water: 1/4 mile lake. Species: Roach, Perch, Carp, Bream, Tench, Rudd. Permits: Day tickets. Charges: Adult £3 per rod or £5 for 2 rods, Children & O.A.Ps £2. Season: 23rd May - 1st April. Methods: No Ground bait, Dog & cat food, Boilies, Barbless hooks only.

Calne

Blackland Lakes

Contact: J or B Walden, Blackland Lakes Holiday & Leisure Centre, Stockley Lane, Calne, Wiltshire, SN11 0NQ, 01249 813672, Water: 1 x 1 acre, 1 x 3/4 acre. Species: Carp (to 30lbs), Tench, Roach, Bream, Perch. Charges: 1 rod £6, extra rods £1, concessions OAP's and children, special rates for campers. Season: Open all year. Methods: Barbless hooks, No ground bait, No large fish or Bream in keep nets.

Cheddar

Blakeway Fisheries

Contact: Mark Durston-Sweet, Blakeway, Nr Wedmore, Somerset BS28 4UB, 01934 712532, Species: Carp, Bream, Tench, Roach & Rudd. Charges: £4 per day. Jun/OAP £2.50.

Cheddar Angling Club

Contact: Cheddar Angling Club, P.O. Box 1183, Cheddar, Somerset BS27 3LT, 01934 744595, Water: 200 acre Cheddar reservoir. Species: Pike, Perch, Tench, Roach, Eels. Permits: Only from: Broadway House Caravan Park, Axbridge Road, Cheddar, Somerset. Bristol Angling Centre, 12-16 Doncaster Road, Southmead, Bristol. Charges: Seniors season permit £30, Juniors season permit £15, Seniors day permit £5, Juniors day permit £3. Season: Tue 16th March 1998 to Sun 14th March 1999 inclusive. Methods: No live baiting, Moderate ground baiting, No dead baiting until 1st July.

Stone Yard Fisheries

Contact: Thatchers Angling, 18 Queen St, Wells, Somerset BA5 2DP, 01749 673513, Water: Small Ponds (15 Anglers) at Chewton Mendip. Species: Carp, Tench. Permits: Only from Thatchers Angling. Charges: Day £5 Senior, £2.50 Junior. Season: March 1st - October 31st. Methods: Barbless hooks.

Chippenham

Chippenham Angling Club

See entry under Avon. Carp Lake.

Ivy House Lakes & Fisheries

Contact: Jo, Ivyhouse Lakes, Grittenham, Chippenham, Wilts, SN15 4JU, 01666 510368, Water: 2 Acre + 6 Acre lakes. Species: Carp, Bream, Roach, Tench, Chub, Perch. Permits: On the bank day tickets, No night fishing. Charges: £6 - two rods, £4 - One rod, £3 Ladies O.A.Ps etc. Season: All year. Methods: Boilies, Tiger nuts banned, Ground bait in moderation.

Sevington Lakes Fishery

Contact: RJ Pope, Wellfield House, Parkhouse Lane, Keynsham, Bristol 0117 9861841, Water: 2.5 acres in 2 lakes, Species: Mirror & Common Carp, Crucians, Roach, Perch, Tench & Rudd, Charges: Day Ticket: Adult £5, Junior £2.50 , Season: Open all year - Dawn to dusk, Methods: Barbless hooks please.

Silverlands Lake

Contact: Mr & Mrs King, Wick Farm, Lacock, Chippenham, Wilts 01249 730244, Water: One spring fed 2 1/2 acre lake. Species: Carp, Tench, Bream. Permits: Only from the fishery. Charges: Day/Night tickets £4, Season tickets 12 months - £80 Adult, £40 Juniors under 16. Season: Open all year. Methods: No dogs please.

Clevedon

Plantations Lake

Contact: Mr or Mrs W.Travis, Middle Lane Farm, Middle Lane, Kingston Seymour, Clevedon, BS21 6XW, 01934 832325, Water: 3/4 acre Carp lake, 2 1/2 acre Coarse lake. Species: 12 Species of coarse fish inc. Barbel, Crucian Carp. 3 Species of Carp in Carp lake. Charges: £5 Adult (£1 extra rod),

£3.50 Juniors, O.A.P.'s, Disabled. 1/2 days available. Season: All year. Methods: No boilies, Barbless hooks, No keep nets (Only for matches).

Devizes

Lakeside
Contact: Miss Harrison or Mrs Gleeb, Devizes Rd, Rowde, Nr Devizes, Wilts 01380 722767, Water: 2 acre lake. Species: Carp, Tench, Roach, Bream, Rudd. Charges: £5 per person 2 rods, £3 disabled / O.A.P's. Season: Open April 1 - October 30, 7a.m. to dusk. Methods: Barbless hooks, No boilies, Unhooking mats to be used, No particle baits (nuts).

Fairford

Milestone Fisheries
Contact: London Road, Fairford, Gloucs GL7 4DS, 01285 713908, Water: 3 1/2 acre - mixed coarse lake. 56 acre Pike lake. Species: Well stocked Carp, Tench, Bream, Roach, Rudd, Perch. Separate Pike lake. Permits: Day tickets available from fishery office - above address. Charges: £5.00 per day (2 rods) Junior £3.00 per day. Pike lake - Day ticket £8, Night ticket £8, Day & Night ticket £13. Season: No closed season, open every day except Dec 25th. Night fishing by arrangement. Pike lake Open from 1st October - End of April, Methods: No keep nets, No dogs, Barbless hooks only. Pike lake - Barbless & semi - barbless hooks - Min of 12lb b.s. line, Traces min 18lbs, 36" soft mesh landing net, Unhooking mat, Strong wire cutters.

Frome

Edneys Fisheries
Contact: Richard Candy, Edneys Farm, Mells, Frome, Somerset 01373 812294, Water: 2 lakes, Species: Carp, Tench etc. Charges: Adults £4.00, Under 14 yrs £2.50.

Mells Pit Pond
Contact: Mr M.Coles, Lyndhurst, Station Road, Mells, Frome 01373 812094, Water: 1 acre. Species: Various Carp, Rudd, Roach, Tench, Perch. Permits: Tickets issued at bankside. Charges: £4 per day. Methods: Barbless hooks.

Frome Angling Association
See entry under River Frome. 10 acre lake.

Highbridge

Emerald Pool Fishery
Contact: Mr Alan Wilkinson, Emerald Pool Fishery, Puriton Road, West Huntspill, Highbridge 01278 794707, Water: 1 1/2 acre lake. Species: Bream, Golden Orfe, Roach, Rudd, Tench, Perch, Carp to 2lb, Sturgeon to 4 feet long. Permits: Environment Agency rod licence required on this water. Charges: £4 per rod, £2 disabled, £3 juniors. Season: All year. Methods: Barbless hooks only, No Carp sacks, No peanuts or ground bait, All Sturgeon to be released immediately, No fish over 3lb to be retained at all.

North Somerset Association of Anglers
Water: See entry under Yeo. 3 coarse ponds.

Kingston Seymour

Bullock Farm Fishing Lakes
Contact: Phillip Simmons, Bullock Farm, Kingston Seymour, Somerset BS21 6XA, 01934 835020, Water: 3 Lakes totalling 3.5 acres, including specialist Carp lake. Species: Carp - Common, Mirror, Ghost, Crucian, Grass, Purple and Koi. Tench, Roach, Rudd, Chub, Bream, Skimmer Bream, Golden Orfe, Golden Tench. Permits: Only at lakeside. Charges: £5.00 day ticket, £3.00 O.A.P's / Under 14s / Disabled. Season tickets & Match rates available. Season: Open all year round Dawn - Dusk. Methods: No boilies, Barbless hooks, No keep nets on Carp lake, No dogs, U14's to be accompanied by an adult, Common sense!

Langport

Thorney Lakes
Contact: Richard or Ann England, Thorney Farm, Muchelney, Langport 01458 250811, Water: Two 2 Acre lakes. , Species: A selection of coarse fish including large Carp. Permits: On the bank. Charges: £4 per day, £2 per 1/2 day after 4 p.m, £2 for O.A.Ps + Children under 16. Season: 16th March - 31st January. Methods: Barbless hooks, No boilies, nuts or pulses, All nets to be dipped on site.

Somerton

Viaduct Fishery
Contact: Mr Robbie Winram (Manager), Viaduct Fishery, Cary Valley, Somerton, Somerset, TA11 6LU, 01458 274022, Water: 5 x Coarse Lakes. Species: Mirror, Crucian + Common Carp, Perch, Roach, Bream, Tench + Golden Tench, Rudd, Ruffe. Permits: Fishing Office or Pre - Payment Office. Charges: Day ticket £5, Shared Peg day £6, Summer Evening ticket £3. Winter Half day ticket £3. Season: All year. Methods: All nets to be dipped, no nuts or boilies, barbless hooks size 8 max, no fixed rigs, ledgers or feeders, no braided hook lengths, fishing from pegs only.

Street

Godney Moor Ponds
Contact: Nick Hughes, Street Angling Centre, 160 High Street, Street, Somerset, BA16 ONH, 01458 447830, Water: Approx. 4 acres. Species: Coarse fish only. Permits: Only from Street Angling Centre. Charges: £3.50 per day (All genders). Season tickets available from 1 April 1998, Methods: No nuts, 2 rods max.

Taunton

Taunton Angling Association
See entry under Taunton and Bridgwater Canal. 4 lakes.

Trowbridge

Rood Ashton Lake
Contact: Marlene Pike, Home Farm, Rood Ashton, Trowbridge, Wilts, BA14 6BG, 01380 870272, Water: 7 acre. Species: Carp, Tench. Permits: Home Farm, Lake View. Charges: 6

a.m. - 6 p.m. £4.50, O.A.P's / Juniors £3.50. 6 p.m. - 11 a.m. £3.50, O.A.P's / Juniors £2.50. Season: Open all year, Methods: (S.R.) No keep nets (only competitions) Tin cans or boilies, Barbless hooks, No nuts.

Warminster

Longleat Lakes & Shearwater
Contact: Nick Robbins, Longleat Estate Office, Longleat, Warminster, Wilts 01985 844496, Water: Longleat 3 Lakes, Top lake Carp up to 25lb, Shearwater 37 acres, Carp up to 25lb. Species: Carp, Roach, Bream, Tench, Perch, Rudd. Permits: From bailiff on the bank. Charges: Adults £5 per day, Children & O.A.Ps £2.50. Season: 1st May - 10th March. Methods: No keep nets or carp sacks, no boilies except Longleat. No nuts, peas, beans on all lakes, no bolt rigs.

Southleigh Lake
Contact: Mr John Shiner at on-site sub Post Office, Crockerton Out Of Town Shopping Centre, Crockerton, Warminster, Wilts 01985 846424, Water: Private 2 acre lake. Species: Mirror, Common Carp, Bream, Roach, Tench. Charges: £3 Day ticket. Season: Mon - Sat 8 a.m. - 7 p.m. * Sunday - matches only (by advanced booking). Methods: Barbless hooks only, No Carp in keep nets, No boilies.

Westbury

Clivey Ponds
Contact: Mr Mike Mortimer, "Lakeside", Clivey, Dilton Marsh, Westbury BA13 4BA, 01373 858311, Water: 1 acre lake, Species: Roach, Rudd, Bream, Perch, Carp, Crucians, Tench and Gudgeon, Permits: Haines Angling Centre, Christchuch St West, Frome. Charges: £3 per Day Ticket. Juniors OAPs etc. £2 per day, Season: All year, Methods: Barbless Hooks Only. No Groundbait

Eden Vale Angling Association
Contact: Mr D Lewis, 3 Monmouth Drive, Frome, Somerset BA11 2DR, 01373 465491, Water: 5 1/2 acre lake, opposite Westbury Station. Species: Common and Mirror Carp, Tench, Bream, Roach, Perch, Pike. Permits: (15 mile radius of Westbury restricted membership) Day tickets: Monday - Friday from Railway Pub - opposite lake. Charges: on application, Season: June 16th - March 15th, Methods: No restrictions on bait, No keep nets until June 16th, Night fishing for full members only.

The Woodland Park
Contact: Mrs S.H.Capon, Brokerswood, Westbury, Wiltshire BA13 4EH, 01373 822238, Water: 5 Acre lake within 80 acre country park. Species: Carp, Roach, Tench, Perch, Dace. Charges: Adults £4, Children £2.75. Season: Closed 20th April - 16th June. Methods: Barbless hooks, No boilies, No keep nets.

Wiveliscombe

Oxenleaze Farm Caravans & Coarse Fishery
Contact: Richard & Marion Rottenbury, Chipstable, Wiveliscombe, Somerset TA4 2QH, 01984 623427, Water: 3 Lakes 1.5 Acres. Species: Carp, Tench, Roach, Rudd,

Bream. Charges: £4.50 Per person per day (2 Rods max). Season: 1 March - 31 October, Methods: Barbless Hooks, No ground bait, No keep nets.

SOUTH WESSEX

RIVER FISHING

THE 'HAMPSHIRE' AVON

The River Avon is one of England's most famous rivers, and is revered by all anglers for the quality of fish that live in it. This river creates a certain mystique that captivates the attentions of fishers from all walks of life.

The River Avon rises in the Vale of Pewsey and, with its tributaries the Bourne and Wylye, drains the chalk of Salisbury plain. The River Nadder, which is joined by the Wylye near Salisbury, drains the escarpment of the South Wiltshire Downs and the Kimmeridge clays of the Wardour Vale. The River Ebble and Ashford Water also drain the South Wiltshire Downs and join the Avon downstream of Salisbury and Fordingbridge respectively.

Below Fordingbridge, a number of streams drain the New Forest area. The Avon finally drains into Christchurch harbour, where it is joined by the Rivers Stour and Mude before discharging into the English Channel.

RIVER AVON PEWSEY - CHRISTCHURCH

Fisheries located between Pewsey and Salisbury are predominantly managed for brown trout fly fishing. A mixture of coarse, salmon and trout fishing is available on the main river between Salisbury and Christchurch.

Avon Springs Fishing Lake
Contact: BJ Bawden, Recreation Road, Durrington, Salisbury, Wiltshire 01980 653557, Water: 1 mile Hampshire Avon at Durrington. Species: Brown Trout + Grayling. Charges: £35 adult, £25 junior. Methods: Fly only.

Christchurch Angling Club
Contact: RJ Andrews, 4 Marley Close, New Milton, Hants BH25 5LL, 01425 638502, Water: Largest club on the river Avon, mainly mid/lower Avon, Fordingbridge - Christchurch, also Fishing on River Stour between Shillingstone and Christchurch plus various coarse ponds. Please telephone the secretary for full details, Species: Roach, Chub, Dace, Barbel, Pike, Bream, Perch, Carp. Permits: From the Secretary or direct from local Tackle Shops. Charges: Adult £80,

Junior £36, Concession £50, (joining fee £15 adult, £6 junior).

Ringwood & District Angling Club
Contact: Mr K J Grozier, 11 Merlin Close, Hightown, Ringwood, Hants, BH24 3RB, 01425 471466, Water: Various stretches on the Hampshire Avon between Burgate and Ringwood (Severals fishery). Species: Roach, Chub, Dace, Barbel, Pike, Bream, Perch, Carp. Salmon, Sea trout, Brown trout. Charges: Adult £75, Junior £37, Con' £55 (joining fee - £15 adult, £5 junior), day tickets £7.50. Prices subject to seasonal review.

Royalty Fishery
Contact: Davis Tackle, 75 Bargates, Christchurch, Dorset 01202 485169, Water: Approx. 1 mile of double bank fishing. Lowest beat on the river. Species: Roach, Chub, Dace, Barbel, Pike, Bream, Perch, Carp, Salmon, Sea Trout, Brown Trout. Charges: Vary with time of year. Methods: No spinning, no night fishing (except for sea trout by arrangement)

Salisbury & District Angling Club
Contact: RW Hillier - Secretary, 29 New Zealand Avenue, Salisbury, Wilts SP2 7JX, 01722 321164, Water: Several stretches on River Avon at Little Durnford, Amesbury, Ratfyn Farm & Countess Water. also on River Wylye, Nadder, Ebble, Bourne & Ratfyn Lake at Amesbury. Species: All species Game and Coarse, Charges: Full or Associate Membership available. Details from the Secretary.

Services Dry Fly Fishing Association
Contact: Major (Retd) CD Taylor - Hon Secretary, c/o G2 Sy Regional Headquarters, 3rd (UK) Division, Picton Barracks, Bulford Camp, Salisbury, SP4 9NY Water: 7 miles on River Avon from Bulford upstream to Fifield, Species: Brown Trout & Grayling, Permits: Fishing Restricted to Serving & Retired members of the Armed Forces. for membership details apply to Secretary, Methods: Only upstream fishing permitted, dry fly exclusively during May & dry fly/ nymph thereafter.

Winkton Fishery
Contact: Davis Tackle, 75 Bargates, Christchurch, Dorset 01202 485169, Water: Approx. 1 mile of fishing. Lower river near Christchurch. Species: Roach, Chub, Dace, Barbel, Pike, Bream, Perch, Carp, Salmon, Sea Trout, Brown Trout. Charges: On application, Methods: No spinning, no night fishing (except for sea trout by arrangement)

Wroughton Angling Club
Contact: Mr T.L.Moulton, 70 Perry's Lane, Wroughton, Swindon, Wilts, SN4 9AP, 01793 813155, Water: 1 1/4 miles Avon and Marden at Chippenham, Reservoir at Wroughton. Species: Roach, Perch, Bream, Pike, Barbel, Chub, Carp, Tench. Permits: Mr L. Hammond - 82 Wharf Road, Wroughton, Wilts. Tel:01793 812031. Charges: £17.50 per season (day tickets £5 seniors). Methods: Restrictions - No Boilies, Peanuts, Particle baits, Dog biscuits, Nuts of any description.

RIVER AXE
Axmouth
Contact: Harbour Services, Harbour Road, Seaton, Devon 01297 22727, Water: Axmouth from lower end Pool below Coly-Axe confluence to Axmouth Bridge, Species: Mullet, Bass, Sea Trout, Permits: Harbour Services. Seaton, Charges: £2.50 Day Adult. £1 Child. £12.50 week Adult. £5 Child. Methods: Fishing from East Bank of Estuary Only.

RIVER WYLYE
The River Wylye rises near Kingston Deverill and flows off chalk, draining the western reaches of Salisbury plain. The river confluences with the River Nadder at Wilton near Salisbury, then joins the main River Avon which flows south to Christchurch.
This river is best described as a 'classic' chalk stream supporting predominantly Brown Trout; hence most fisheries here are managed for fly fishermen. The fishing is predominantly controlled by local syndicates and estates.

Langford Fisheries
Contact: Paul Knight or Allan Walton, Duck Street, Steeple Langford, Salisbury, Wiltshire 01722 790770, Water: Wylye - 1 mile. Species: Brown trout, Grayling. Charges: £25 - 2 fish limit plus catch and release, Grayling fishing £15 per day catch & release. Season: April 15th - Oct 15th, Oct 15th - March 14th Fly only.

Sutton Veny Estate
Contact: Mr & Mrs A.Walker, Eastleigh Farm, Bishopstrow, Warminster, Wiltshire 01985 212325. Water: 4 miles on River Wylye. Species: Brown trout. Charges: £50 per day per beat (600yds). Season: 15th April - 15th Oct. Methods: Dry fly & upstream nymph only.

RIVER NADDER
The River Nadder rises near Tisbury draining the escarpment of the South Wiltshire Downs and Kimmeridge Clay of the Wardour Vale. The River Wylye joins the Nadder near Wilton before entering the main River Avon at Salisbury.
The Nadder is well known as a mixed fishery of exceptional quality; there is a diverse array of resident species including Chub, Roach, Dace, Bream, Pike, Perch, Brown Trout and Salmon. Much of the fishing is controlled by estates and syndicates although two angling clubs offer some access to the river.

Tisbury Angling Club
Contact: Mr E.J.Stevens, Knapp Cottage, Fovant, Salisbury, Wiltshire 01722 714245, Water: 2 miles on River Nadder. Species: Roach, Chub, Dace, Pike, Bream, Perch, Carp, Brown trout. Charges: Adult £24, Junior £6, Con' £10.

Kennet and Avon Canal
A relatively small section of this canal falls within the South Wessex area

RIVER STOUR

The River Stour in Dorset is well known by anglers across the country for quality of its fishing. Over the years many British record captures have been made here, for example the current roach record stands at 4lb 3oz, taken from the Stour near Wimborne.
The Stour rises on the Greensand at St Peters Pump in Stourhead Gardens and flows through Gillingham near by where it is joined by the Shreen Water and the River Lodden. The Stour stretches for 96 km, passing through the Blackmoor Vale down to the sea at Christchurch; the total fall over this distance is approximately 230 m. Other notable tributaries along its length include the River Tarrant confluencing near Spetisbury, the River Allen at Wimborne and the Moors River coming in near Christchurch. The Stour confluences with the River Avon at the 'Clay Pool' in Christchurch, before flowing into the harbour area and ultimately out into the English Channel.

Christchuch Angling Club
See entry under Avon

Blandford & District Angling Club
Contact: Mr V Claydon (sec), 8 Jubilee Way, Blandford Forum, Dorset DT11 7UW, 01258 456345, Water: 4 miles of Dorset Stour. Species: Roach, Bream, Perch, Carp, Chub, Pike etc. Permits: Conyers Tackle Shop, Market Place, Blandford. Charges: Senior £25, O.A.P £15, Junior £8, Day tickets £3. Season: Normal coarse season. Methods: Boilies banned.

Dorchester & District Angling Society
Contact: J Parkes, 5 Malta Close, Dorchester, Dorset DT1 1QT, 01305 262813, Water: 3 miles on Dorset Stour, 1.5 miles Dorset Frome plus 1 lake Toller Porcorum, Species: Roach, Dace, Chub, Pike, Gudgeon, Perch, Eels, Permits: Anglers Tackle Store, Weymouth. Revels Tackle, Dorchester. Charges: £32 senior, £16 Senior citizen, £16 Junior, Season: June 16th - March 14th. Stillwater open all year.

Durweston Angling Association
Contact: Mr Vernon Bell (secretary), "Endcote", Durweston 01258 451317, Water: 2 miles River Stour, 2 acre lake, (including Weir & Mill Pool). Species: Carp in lake, Bream, Roach, Rudd, Gudgeon, Dace, Eels, Chub, Pike, Perch. Permits: "The White Horse" Public house, Stour Paine. The Mill House, Durweston (after 9 a.m.). Charges: Day tickets: River £3, Lake £6. Joint lake and river permit £41. Season: Close season 14th March - 16th June, Lake open all year. Methods: Lake: No boilies, beans or trout pellets. barbless hooks.

Gillingham & District AA
Contact: Simon Hebditch (Hon. Secretary), 5 Ham Court, Shaftsbury Rd, Gillingham, Dorset, SP8 4LU, 01747 824817, Water: 7 miles Upper Stour - Gillingham to Marnhull. Turners Paddock lake at Stourhead. Mappowder Court 4 lakes at Mappowder. Species: River: Roach, Chub, Dace, Perch, Pike, Gudgeon, Bream. Turners Paddock: Bream, Tench. Mappowder: Carp, Crucians,

Rudd, Tench, Perch. Permits: The Timepiece, Newbury, Gillingham, Dorset, SP8 4HZ. Tel: 01747 823339. Mr P Stone (Treasurer). Charges: £4 day ticket for any water. Membership about £22, Juniors £11. Season: River & Turners Paddock closed in usual close season, Mappowder Court open all year. Methods: Barbless hooks only at Mappowder.

Salisbury & District AA
Contact: RW Hillier - Secretary, 29 New Zealand Avenue, Salisbury, Wilts 01722 321164, Water: 2 Stretches on Stour near Wimbourne, also fishing on River Avon (Salisbury), Avon (Charford), Avon (Durrington), Nadder, along with Petersfinger, Steeple Langford and Wellow Lakes. Species: All species Coarse and Game, Charges: Full membership available to all persons living within 14 mile radius of Salisbury. Associate membership available outside this area. Details from the secretary.

Stalbridge Angling Association
Contact: Mrs D Fletcher, Corner Cottage, High Street, Stalbridge DT10 2LH, 01963 362025, Water: 2 1/2 miles Stour, 3 ponds. Species: Bream, Tench, Roach, Dace, Pike, Chub, Carp, Rudd. Permits: Ring St Filling Station, Ring St, Stalbridge. Charges: Senior Annual £15 + £5 joining fee, Junior £5.50 + No joining fee. Methods: No boilies on ponds.

Sturminster & Hinton A.A
Contact: R.Wylde, 10 Hillside, Manston, Sturminster Newton, Dorset, DT10 1EY, 01258 473391, Water: 14 miles mid River Stour, 3 small lakes (members only). Species: Roach, Chub, Tench, Bream, Perch, Carp, Pike. Permits: Harts Garden Supplies, Kevs Autos or S. Dimmer (Membership Secretary) 01963 363291. Charges: £3 day, £10 per week, Juniors £2 per year, Adults £15 + £5 joining fee. Season: March 14th - June 16th. Methods: No dogs, Radios, No live baiting, No night fishing, One rod, second rod for Pike only.

Throop Fisheries
See entry under Coarse Fisheries - Bournemouth. 10 miles on Dorset Stour.

Wareham & District Angling Society
Contact: Mary Spiller, G.Elmes & Son, St Johns Hill, Wareham, Dorset. BH20 4NB, 01929 552623, Water: River waters on North Dorset Stour and the Frome. 3 lakes Wareham area, Species: Coarse. Permits: Wessex Angling, Poole, Dorset. Charges: Senior £32, Ladies / O.A.P's £16, Junior £15, (subject to confirmation). Season: One lake open during Coarse closed season. Methods: Barbless, No litter, No cans, Variations as per membership book.

Wimbourne & District Angling Club
Contact: G.E.Pipet (secretary), 12 Seatown Close, Canford Heath, Poole 01202 382123, Water: 10 miles River Stour, 15 lakes. Species: Trout & Coarse Fisheries. Permits: Certain waters are available on Guest Tickets £5 from Wessex Angling, 321 Wimborne Rd, Oakdale, Poole. Charges: £50 + £8 joining fee. Methods: Barbless hooks on Coarse stillwaters, No floating baits.

RIVER FROME

The Frome rises through chalk on the North Dorset Downs near Evershot, and flows south through Dorchester, and finally Wareham, where it confluences with the River Piddle in Poole harbour.
The River Frome is well known for its excellent salmon, brown trout and grayling fishing. There are also good numbers of coarse fish in certain areas; although access is limited sport can be very rewarding. Salmon and trout fishing is generally controlled by syndicates and local estates.

Dorchester Fishing Club
Contact: Mr J.Grindle, 36 Cowleaze, Martinstown, Dorset DT2 9TD, 01305 889682, Water: Approx. 6.5 miles of double bank on the Frome near Dorchester, Brown trout fly fishing. Species: Brown trout, Grayling. Permits: John Aplin, Dorchester (01305) 266500. Charges: Adult £235 (day permit £20). Season: April 1st - Oct 14th. Methods: Dry fly and Nymph only.

Frome, Piddle & West Dorset Fishery Association
Contact: Mr PJ Leatherdale, Hanthorpe Cottage, Briantspuddle, Dorchester, Dorset, DT2 HR, 01305 265252, Water: An amalgamation of riparian owners with an interest in the welfare of river fisheries in their locality. Information can be obtained concerning estate waters from the contact above.

Wessex Fly Fishing & Chalk Streams Ltd.
Water: See entry under Piddle & Frome

RIVER PIDDLE AND WEST DORSET STREAMS

'West Dorset' streams include the river Brit, Asker, Bride and Char. These streams are relatively short, 'steep' water courses supporting populations of mainly brown trout and sea trout.
The River Piddle rises at four major springs near Alton St Pancras, initially flowing south before turning east at Puddletown towards Poole Harbour, where it confluences with the River Frome. This is a relatively small river known primarily for its Salmon, Brown Trout and Sea Trout. Other fish species can be found in the River Piddle including, Roach, Dace, Pike and Perch. Much of the fishing is controlled by local syndicates and estate waters; further information about these groups can be obtained from the aforementioned Frome, Piddle and West Dorset Fishery Association.

Environment Agency
Contact: Recreation Officer, Environment Agency, Rivers House, Sunrise Business Park, Blandford Forum, Dorset DT11 8ST. 01258 456080 Water: 3km of bank fishing on lower Piddle. Species: Salmon & Sea Trout. Charges: £250 plus vat (£293.75, subject to annual review).

Wessex Fly Fishing & Chalk Streams Ltd
Contact: Richard Slocock, Lawrences Farm, Tolpuddle, Dorchester, Dorset 01305 848460, Water: 5 Lakes & Pools Totalling 4 acres for Rainbow Trout. Plus 16 Beats on Rivers Piddle & Frome for Brown Trout. Charges: Rivers: Minimum £15 day. Max £49. Season: Rivers: April 1st to October 15th. Methods: Fly Fishing only. Most river beats are catch & release using barbless hooks.

STILLWATER TROUT

Beaminster

Knights in the Bottom Lakes
Contact: Jill Haynes, Knights in the Bottom, Hooke, Beaminster, Dorset, DT8 3PG, 01308 862157, Water: 3 Lakes, 3.5 acres of water. Species: Trout. Charges: On application. Season: April - October. Methods: Fly Only.

Bridport

Mangerton Mill
Contact: Mr Harris, Mangerton Mill, Mangerton, Bridport, Dorset, DT6 3SG, 01308 485224, Water: 1 Acre lake. Species: Rainbow Trout. Permits: At mill. Season: 1st April - 31st December. Methods: Max hook size 10.

Christchurch

Christchurch Angling Club
Contact: RJ Andrews, 4 Marley Close, New Milton, Hants BH25 5LL, 01425 638502, Water: Largest club on the river Avon, mainly mid/lower Avon, Fordingbridge - Christchurch, also Fishing on River Stour between Shillingstone and Christchurch. Stillwater Game fishing at Cranebrook and other stillwaters. Sea Trout at Christchurch Harbour. Please telephone the secretary for full details, Species: Salmon, Sea Trout & Brown Trout, Permits: From the Secretary, or direct from local Tackle shops. Charges: Adult £80, Junior £36, Concession £50, (joining fee £15 adult, £6 junior).
See also entry under River Fishing - Avon

Cranborne

Wimbourne & District Angling Club
Water: See entry River Stour. Various local lakes.

Dorchester

Flowers Farm Fly Fishers
Contact: Alan.J.Bastone, Flowers Farm, Hilfield, Dorchester, DT2 7BA. 01300 341351. Water: 5 lakes total 3.75 acres. Species: Rainbow & Brown trout. Charges: £18 day, £14 half day, £10.50 evening. Season: Open all year 5.30am to dusk. Methods: Single fly, Max size 10, Bank fishing only.

Hermitage Lakes
Contact: Nigel Richardson, Common Farm, Hermitage, Cerne Abbas, Dorchester 01963 210556, Water: 3 half acre lakes. Species:

Rainbow & Brown trout. Charges: Day (4 fish) £14, Halfday (3 fish) £11, Evening (2 fish) £8. Season: Open all season. Methods: Max size 10 longshank.

Pallington Lakes
Contact: Mrs Clarke, Tincleton, Dorchester, Dorset 01305 848141, Water: 5 Acre Trout lake. Species: Rainbow Trout.

Wessex Fly Fishing & Chalk Streams Ltd
Water: See entries under Piddle and Frome. 5 clearwater lakes and pools totalling 4 acres. Charges: Lakes: Day £23. 1/2 day £19. Eve £14. Season: Lakes: March 1st - Jan 15th.

Fordingbridge

Damerham Fisheries
Contact: Mike Davies, The Lake House, Damerham, Fordingbridge, Hants, SP6 3HW, 01725 518446, Water: 6 lakes. 1.5 mile Allan River. Species: Rainbow Trout (Blue Rainbow Trout). Permits: Season Rods. Charges: Full Rod £1,260.00 (30 days), 1/2 Rod £630 (15 days), 1/4 Rod £420 (10 days). Season: March - October. Methods: Fly only.

Rockboune Trout Fishery
Contact: Rockbourne Trout Fishery, Rockbourne Road, Sandleheath, Fordingbridge, Hampshire, SP6 1QG, 01725 518603, Water: 6 Spring fed lakes & 3 chalkstream beats on the Sweatford water. Species: Rainbow & Brown Trout. Permits: From the fishery. Charges: Day ticket 5 fish limit £32, Half day 4 fish limit £28, Half day 3 fish limit £23, Evening ticket 2 fish limit £17, Stream beats day ticket £25. Season: Commencing 15th March. Methods: Fly only.

Lyme Regis

Amherst Lodge
Contact: Andrew Bryceson, Amherst Lodge, Uplyme, Lyme Regis, Dorset, DT7 3XH, 01297 442773, Water: 4 stream fed Trout lakes. Species: Rainbow & Brown. Permits: Go to rod room on arrival. Charges: Day ticket, 4 fish limit £18, Half day, 3 fish limit £14. Season: Open all year, Dawn to dusk, Must book if arriving before 8.00 a.m. Methods: All conventional methods acceptable, No spinning, Bait etc.

Salisbury

Avon Springs Fishing Lake
Contact: BJ Bawden, Recreation Road, Durrington, Salisbury, Wiltshire 01980 653557, Water: One 4 acre lake, One 3 acre lake. Species: Brown Trout + Rainbow Trout, Charges: £30 per day, £19 junior. 1/2 day £23, junior £15, £16 eve. Season: Open all year 8.30am to dusk, Methods: Fly only no lures.

Langford Fisheries
Contact: Paul Knight or Allan Walton, Duck Street, Steeple Langford, Salisbury, Wiltshire 01722 790770, Water: 12 acre Trout lake. Species: Rainbow, few Brown trout. Permits: From fishery. Charges: Day ticket £27 - 4 fish or £30 - 4 fish plus catch & release, £18 - 2 fish. Boats £70 - 4 fish each plus catch & release. Season: Open all year. Methods: Max size 10 hook.

Stockbridge

John O ' Gaunts
Contact: Mrs E Purse, 51 Mead Road, Chandlers Ford, Hants SO53 2FB, 01703 252268, Water: 2 Lakes approx. 7 acres in Test Valley, Species: Rainbow Trout, Permits: Available from Fishery Tel: 01703 252268 or 01794 388130, Charges: £28 Day - 4 fish, £16 1/2 day - 2 Fish, Season: February 1st - November 30th inclusive, Methods: Fly and Nymph only.

STILLWATER COARSE

There are many lakes and ponds in the area with access for coarse anglers; some of these are controlled by angling clubs already mentioned in this guide. A selection of other stillwater coarse fisheries across the South Wessex area are summarised below.
The Environment Agency owns a small pond near Wimborne with permit access for anglers. Facilities include a small picnic area, a toilet and access for disabled anglers in wheel chairs.

Blandford

Durweston Angling Association
See entry under Stour. 2 acre lake.

Bournemouth

Throop Fisheries
Contact: Glen Sutcliffe, South Lodge, Holdenhurst Village, Bournemouth 01202 395532, Water: 10 Miles of river bank on Dorset Stour + Stillwater Mill Pool. Species: Barbel, Chub, Carp, Roach, Tench, Perch, Dace, Pike. Charges: £6.50 Adult One rod, Two rods £9.00. Season: 16th June - 14 March (Open every day between these dates). Methods: No night fishing.

Christchurch

Avon Tyrrell Lakes
Contact: Richard Bonney, Avon Tyrrell House, Bransgore, Christchurch BH23 8EE, 01425 672347, Water: Two lakes totalling approx. 2.5 acres, Species: Carp, Tench, Roach, Bream, Perch and Rudd, Permits: On site from reception. Charges: £5 Day Tickets Adults. £2.50 Juniors(Under 16). Season Tickets also available, please note Night Fishing only available on a season ticket, Season: Open mid June to Mid March 8am to 8pm, Methods: Barbless Hooks, No keep nets, No nut baits. See rules on site.

Christchurch Angling Club
See entry under River Fishing - Avon

Whirlwind Lake
Contact: Mr & Mrs Pillinger, Whirlwind Rise, Dudmore Lane, Christchurch, Dorset, BH23 6BQ, 01202 475255, Water: Secluded lake. Species: Common, Crucian and Mirror Carp, Roach, Rudd, Tench, Chub etc. Permits: On site and local fishing tackle shops. Advanced

booking advisable. Charges: Adults £8 per day (Limited places). Season: Open all year. Methods: Barbless hooks only. No keep nets, No boilies.

Cranborne

Gold Oak Fishery
Contact: Mr J Butler, Gold Oak Farm, Hare Lane, Cranborne, Dorset 01275 517275, Water: 7 small lakes. Species: Carp, Green + Golden Tench, Perch, Roach, Chub, Bream. Charges: Summer day - £7 Adult, £5 Junior, 1/2 day - £5 Adult, £3 Junior, Eve - £3 Adult, £1 Junior. Winter day - £5 Adult, £3 Junior, 1/2 day - £3 Adult, £2 junior. Season: All year. Methods: No large fish in keep nets, Barbless hooks, Dogs on lead.

Martins Farm Fishery
Contact: Mr Ball, Martins Farm, Woodlands, Nr Verwood, Dorset 01202 822335, Water: 2.5 acre spring fed lake, Species: Carp, Tench, Perch, Roach. Charges: £6 day ticket, £3.50 juniors, £5 OAP's, Season: Closed 16 March - 16 June. Open: Mon, Wed, Sat & Sun Methods: No keep nets, Barbless hooks, No Boilies, Unhooking mats preferred

Wimbourne & District Angling Club
See entry under Stour. Various local ponds.

Crewkerne

Highlands Dairy Lake
Contact: J.Wyatt, Highlands Dairy Farm, Hewish, Nr Crewkerne, Somerset 01460 74180, Water: 1 acre lake. Species: Carp, Tench, Rudd, Roach, Perch. Permits: At house. Charges: £4 per day. Season: Open all year. Methods: No keep nets for Carp.

Dorchester

Dorchester & District Angling Society
Contact: Mr J.Parkes, 5 Malta Close, Dorchester, Dorset DT1 1QT, 01305 262813, Water: See entry under Stour. One coarse lake at Toller Porcorum.

Hermitage Lakes
Contact: Nigel Richardson, Common Farm, Hermitage, Cerne Abbas, Dorchester 01963 210556, Water: 1/2 acre lake. Species: Carp. Charges: Day ticket £4. Season: Closed 14th March - 16th June. Methods: Barbless hooks, No keep nets.

Luckfield Lake Fishery
Contact: John Aplin, 1 Athelstan Road, Dorchester, Dorset DT1 1NR, 01305 266500, Water: 1.5 acre clay pit in beautiful surroundings. Species: Carp - 23lb, Tench - 9lb+, Roach - 3lb+. Permits: As above. Charges: Day £5, Night £6, 1/2 season £30, Full season £60. Season: 16 June - 14 Mar. Methods: No keep nets, Barbless hooks.

Pallington Lakes
Contact: Micheal Willard, Pallington, Dorchester DT2 8QV, 01305 848141, Water: 3 lakes. Species: Carp, Tench, Perch, Roach, Bream, Chub. Permits: At above. Charges: Specialist Carp & Tench Lake £7 per day, Evening £4. Coarse lake £6 per day, Evening £3. Season: 1st May - 14th March (Open Easter). Methods: Barbless hooks, No keep nets.

Fordingbridge

New Forest Water Park
Contact: Mark Jury, Hucklesbrook Lakes, Ringwood Road, Fordingbridge, Hants, SP6 2EY, 01425 656868, Water: 19 acre lake, 11 acre lake. Species: Pike to 35lb + Carp to 40lb in 11 acre lake. Carp to 32lb, Tench to 10lb, Roach to 3lb, Rudd to 2lb in 19 acre lake. Permits: From Clubhouse (After 9 a.m.) or on bank. Charges: £5 for 2 rods day ticket, £15 for 24hrs. Season: All year round. Methods: Barbless hooks, No nut baits, No keep nets, No live bait.

Gillingham

Gillingham & District AA
See entry under Stour. 5 lakes.

Lyme Regis

Amherst Lodge
Contact: Andrew Bryceson, Amherst Lodge, Uplyme, Lyme Regis, Dorset, DT7 3XH, 01297 442773, Water: 2 Senior Lakes + 1 Lake for Juniors. Species: Mirror and Common carp to double figures, Tench, Rudd and Roach. Permits: Go to Rod Room on arrival. Charges: Senior lakes day ticket £4.50 (Single rod). Junior ticket £2.50. , Season: Open all year, dawn to dusk, must book if arriving before 8.00am. Methods: Barbless hooks, No keep nets, No nuts. Everything else acceptable in moderation.

Wood Farm Caravan Park
Contact: Ian Pointing, Axminster Road, Charmouth, Dorset DT6 6BT, 01297 560697, Water: 2 ponds totalling approx. 1 acre. Species: Carp, Rudd, Roach, Tench & Perch, Permits: Rod Licences sold, Charges: £3.25 day ticket. Season: All year, Methods: No boilies, keepnets. Barbless hooks only

Salisbury

Langford Fisheries
Contact: Paul Knight or Allan Walton, Duck Street, Steeple Langford, Salisbury, Wiltshire 01722 790770, Water: 7 acre lake. Species: Carp, Tench, Roach, Perch, Pike. Permits: On site. Charges: £6 per day, Concessions & Children £4. Season: Open June 16th - April 30th. Methods: No boilies or nut baits, No Carp in keep nets. Barbless hooks.

Salisbury & District Angling Club
See entry under Avon. Peters Finger Lakes, Steeple Langford and Wellow.

Waldens Farm Fishery
Contact: David & Jackie Wateridge, Waldens Farm, Walden Estate, West Grimstead, Salisbury, Wiltshire, SP5 3RJ, 01722 710480, Water: 5 Lakes for approx. 10 acres. Species: All coarse fish. Permits: From the bank. Charges: Day (dawn to dusk) tickets Adult £6, Junior - O.A.P £4, Evenings 5 p.m. on £3.50, Match peg fees £4. Season: Open full 12 months. Methods: Barbless / Micro barb hooks, No Keepnets, Net dips to be used, No Groundbait, No boilies, nuts or cereals.

Witherington Farm Fishing
Contact: Tony or Caroline Beeny, New Cottage, Witherington Farm, Downton,

Salisbury, SP5 3QX, 01722 710021, Water: 3 Well stocked lakes. Species: Carp, Tench, Roach, Bream, Rudd, Chub, Perch. Permits: On bank. Charges: Full day £5, Half day £3, Full day Junior U16 / Disabled / O.A.P £3. Season: All year Dawn - Dusk. Methods: No Boilies, Barbless hooks, All nets to be dipped, No night fishing, No keep nets only in matches.

Stalbridge

Stalbridge Angling Association
See entry under Stour. 3 ponds.

Sturminster Newton

Sturminster & Hinton A.A.
See entry under Stour. 3 small lakes (members only),

Wareham

Wareham & District Angling Society
See entry under Stour. 3 lakes.

Wimbourne

Environment Agency - Canford Pond
Contact: Recreation Officer, Environment Agency, Rivers House, Sunrise Business Park, Blandford Forum, Dorset DT11 8ST. 01258 456080. Water: approx. 2 acres. Species: Carp, Bream, Roach, Perch, Tench, Rudd, Pike. Charges: Adult £40, Conc. £20, Junior £20 (subject to annual review).

Weymouth

Osmington Mills Holidays
Contact: Reception, Osmington Mills, Weymouth, Dorset DT3 6HB, 01305 832311, Water: 1 Acre Lake. Species: Carp, Tench, Bream, Roach. Permits: Caravan Park reception, on bank. Charges: £4 per day Adults, £2.50 under 16, £2.50 Evening ticket after 5 p.m. Season: May 23rd - March 15th. Methods: Barbless hooks, No keep nets, No particle bait.

Radipole Lake
Contact: Mr D.Tattersall, Municipal Offices, North Quay, Weymouth, Dorset, DT4 8TA, 01305 206234, Water: 70 acres plus. Species: Carp to 20lb, Eels, Roach, Dace, Mullett. Permits: Anglers Tackle Store, 64 Park Street, Weymouth, 01305 782624. Charges: Day Junior £1.55, Adult £3.50, 60+ £2.40. Monthly & annual available. Season: 16th June - 14th March. Methods: 2 Rod max, Barbless hooks only, No bivvies.

If you would like an entry in next years directory please write with details to: PO Box 59, Bideford, Devon EX39 4YN.

Advertisers Index

COARSE

GAME

Advertisers Index

Advertisers Index

Advertisers Index

Casting a fly on the River Avon. Picure - Matt Carter

Directions

Game

1. Amherst Lodge
From the A35 Bridport to Honiton road, turn down the B3165 towards Lyme Regis at the Hunter's Lodge Pub. After 1.3 miles turn right down a small road called "Cathole Lane". Keep going round to the right and you will come to Amherst Lodge.

2. Arundell Arms Hotel
Leave the A30 Dual Carriageway east of Launceston and follow signs for Lifton. The Arundell Arms is in the centre of the Village.

3. Bellbrook Valley Trout Fishery
From Tiverton roundabout on A361 head towards Barnstaple. Take 3rd right (6 Miles) signposted Bellbrook & Spurway. Continue down lane for 2 miles then sharp right signed "To the fishery" then 200yds on the right.

From Oakford leave uphill, bear left at Pinkworthy Post (sign posted Rackenford). Follow lane down hill, cross stream then fork left. Fishery 200yds on right.

4. Blakewell Fishery
Take A39 from Barnstaple towards Lynton. 1.5 miles from Barnstaple turn left on to B3230 and follow signs to the fishery.

5. Braggs Wood Trout Fishery
Take the Bude road out of Launceston (B 3254). In the village of Ladycross, take the road to Boyton. Follow signs to Boyton Nurseries (Approx 5 miles from Launceston).

6. Bridge House Hotel
Bridge House Hotel Fishing is on the A396 7 miles west of Tiverton 0.5mile past Oakford Bridge. Please telephone 01398 331298.

7. Bristol Water Fisheries
a Barrows. b Blagdon. c Chew. Bristol Water fisheries are well signposted from major roads. Telephone (01275) 332339 for further details.

8. Cameley Lakes - Temple Cloud
1/2 Mile off A37 Temple Cloud. Road marked Cameley Hinton Blewitt.

9. Carnarvon Arms Hotel
Take junction 27 off M5 following A361 west to Tiverton, follow Dulverton signs on A396.

10. Clifford Farm
A39 Bideford/Clovelly road. Between Clovelly roundabout and Milky Way Farm take the road south signposted Woolfardisworthy At the second turning right, signposted Clifford, follow road for 1.5 miles.

11. Deer Park Hotel
Buckerell Village, Nr Honiton. Devon. Please telephone (01404) 41266 for details

12. Drakelands
From Exeter take the main road to Plympton. At Newnham Industrial Estate take the Cornwood Road to Hemerdon Village. Turn right past Miners Arms, the fishery is signposted 0.75 miles on the left.

13. Drift Resevoir
Take A30 towards Lands End. In Drift village, turn right (signposted "Sancreed"). Reservoir car park is approx 1/4 mile along this lane. Ticket sales enquiries: Adjacent.

14. Environment Agency Fisheries
a Exe & Creedy fisheries. b Watersmeet & Glenthorne fisheries. Directions are supplied with permits.

15. Exe Valley Fishery
M5 exit 27 to Tiverton on A361. Take A396 towards Minehead at Black Cat Junction, continue on A396 towards Minehead, at Exebridge turn left at garage on B3222, over bridge at the Anchor Inn take first right to fishery.

16. Flowers Farm Fly Fishers
Off A337 take Batcombe turning follow St Francis Friary signs. Approx 3 miles off A37. Off A352 take Hilfield Road. Follow Friary signs. Approx 4 miles of A352. Flowers Farm is next to St Francis Friary.

17. Fosfelle Country Manor
Please telephone (01237) 441273 for directions.

18. Fox & Hounds Hotel
From M5 junction 30 take the A377. The Hotel is situated just off the A377 road midway between Exeter & Barnstaple at Eggesford.

19. Goodiford Mill Fishery
From Cullompton take the Honiton road, continue for over a mile past Horns cross. Turn left at signpost for Wressing, Goodiford, Dead lane. Turn right at end of lane, we are on your left.

20. Half Moon Hotel
Sheepwash lies 1 mile North of Highampton (A3072) between Hatherleigh & Holsworthy

21. Half Stone Sporting Agency
Please telephone (01647) 24643 for directions.

22. Highbullen Hotel
Please telephone (01769) 540561 for directions

23. Higher Cownhayne Farm
Please phone for directions. 01297 552267.

24. Hollies Trout Farm
From Cullompton or Honiton take the A373 and follow signs for Sheldon.

25. Innis Country Club
Take A30 to roundabout west of Bodmin, take first exit signposted Bugle. Turn left at Bugle traffic lights and follow road to Penwithick. Turn left again signposted Luxulyan follow road for 1 mile. Fishery signposted on the left.

26. Lifton Hall
Please telephone (01566) 784263 for directions

27. Mill End Hotel
From Exeter exit M5 on to A30. Turn off on A382 and continue driving for approx 15 mins. We are on your right.

Directions

28. Mill Leat Trout Lakes (Thornbury)
Take the A388 North from Holsworthy. Turn right following signs for Thornbury. The fishery is half a mile past Thornbury church.

29. Mill Leat Trout Farm (Ermington)
Take A38 dual carriageway to Ivybridge, then follow Ermington signs (B3211). We are 1st property after Ermington village sign.

30. Newhouse Fishery
From Totnes take the A381 south towards Kingsbridge. After 5 miles turn right to Moreleigh on the B3207. After 2 miles turn right down the lane signposted Newhouse Farm Fishery.

31. Rose Park Fishery
8 miles west of Launceston on the A30 turn off and follow signs for Altarnun. Drive through the village over the bridge and take next right. Follow the road, Rose Park is on the right.

32. South Hay
At Brandis Corner on the A3072 Hatherleigh-Holsworthy road, turn right for Shebbear(4 miles). 0.5 mile from village the main road bends sharply, take minor road straight ahead. At T junction turn left, and left again into our drive.

33. South West Water - Game
a Kennick, b Siblyback, c Wimbleball, d Fernworthy, e Colliford, f Roadford, g Burrator, h Stithians, i Crowdy, j Wistlandpound, k Lower Tamar, l Meldon, m Avon Dam, n Venford. South West Water fisheries are well signposted from major roads.

34. Stafford Moor Fishery
Clearly signposted on the B3220 3 miles North of Winkleigh, 9 miles south of Torrington.

35. Tavistock Trout Fishery
Entrance on A386 one mile from Tavistock.

36. Temple Trout Fishery
Traveling from Bodmin to Launceston along the A30 take the first Temple turning on the right . Travel along this road over a chain ridge at the bottom of the hill, fishery entrance is just a little way along on the left. Travelling from Launceston to Bodmin along the A30 take second Temple turning at T junction, at the end of this road turn right back towards A30. The fishery is 300m on right.

37. Tredethick Farm Cottages
Please phone 01208 873618 for details.

38. Tree Meadow Trout Fishery
Leave the main A30 into Hayle at roundabout, take B3302 Helston road for 4 miles until you reach Fraddam village. Turn left at Deveral road. Fishery one mile on right.

39. Upper Yealm Fishery
We are 1.5 miles north of Lee Mill village. Leave A38 at Lee Mill Exit. In village opposite Westward Inn turn into New Park Road, after 0.5 mile turn right signposted Venton. At each of two signposted junctions follow Cornwood. 500 yards beyond Graze Alders Farm opposite road sign 'Hump backed bridge' turn into open driveway and park close to garage at corner of field on left.

40. Valley Springs
Follow official tourist signs from Frogmore or Totnes Rd, we are half a mile from Cider Press.

41. Viaduct Trout Fishery
From Yeovil take the A37 north towards Ilchester and then the B3151 to Somerton. Turn left onto the B3153 (Signposted Somerton) and go up hill to mini roundabout. Go straight over roundabout and take first right through housing estate to T - junction. Turn left and almost immediately first right onto track to fishery.

42. Watercress Fishery
Signposted from the B3344 Exeter to Chudleigh road just the Exeter side of the Highwaymans Haunt Inn.

43. Wessex Fly Fishing School
In Tolpuddle turn off A35 signed Southover. You will see our signs 0.250 mile along lane.

44. Wessex Water - Game
a Clatworthy. b Hawkridge. c Sutton Bingham. Please telephone 0845 600 2 600 for further details.

45. Wiscombe Park Fishery
Leave the A30 at Honiton. Take A375 towards Sidmouth. turn left at the Hare & Hounds crossroads towards Seaton. After 3 miles turn left towards Blackbury Camp. Fishery signposted first on the left.

Coarse

1. Abbey Coarse Fishery
Take A 367 Bath - Radstock Shepton Mallet Road. Between Radstock - Stratton on Fosse take the B3139 road to Charlton off the white post roundabout. In Charlton Village take the turning to Holcombe. Look for the Holcombe Village sign, just before village turn right. Immediately before it to Moores Farm. Fishery sign on road.

2. Anglers Eldorado
Turn off A30 westbound into Okehampton on B3260. 1 mile after Okehampton take B3079 to Holsworthy & Bude. Carry on for 11 miles to Halwill Junction. Take first right after Garage signposted Anglers El Dorado.

3. Ashcombe Lakes
From Exeter: at end of M5 fork left on A380 for 2mls. Turn left on B3192. After roundabout follow Teignmouth road for 1 mile then left at Ashcombe sign. From Plymouth: at Exeter Racecourse turn left - then under bridge to join A380. Turn right as above. From Torquay: 3 miles after Newton Abbot turn left under bridge crossing A380. Turn right to B3192.

4. Ashmead Lake
2 Miles from the A303 near Martock in Somerset.

Directions

5. Badham Farm
From Looe: Take road to Duloe. At Sandplace before crossing Railway Bridge take small road not signposted on right. Badham Farm about 1 mile on right.
From Liskeard: Take road to St keyne, through village, just before church take left turn sign to St Keyne Well & Badham. About 1 mile on left past Wellhouse Hotel.

6. Bake Lakes
Head towards Trerulefood roundabout (A38). Take Bake exit at roundabout then first right followed by first left. Fishery entrance 0.25mile on right.

7. Bakers Farm
Approx 0.75 miles from Torrington on the B3232 to Barnstaple. Bakers Farm is signposted on the right.

8. Billingsmoor Farm
Approx. 3.5 mls from Tiverton, .75 mls from Butterleigh on the Silverton road, 3.5 miles from Cullompton, 1 mile from Bunniford Cross on the Silverton Road and 3 miles from Silverton on the Butterleigh Road.

9. Bitterwell Lake
M32 then onto A432. From Frenchay traffic lights straight on to next roundabout, turn left heading for Yate. At next roundabout straight across heading for Westerleigh. Last roundabout turn left for Westerleigh past Folly Pub over motorway bridge to crossroads signposted Bitterwell Lake Henfield Road, continue for 300 yards into Ram Hill. Lake 200yards on right.

10. Blackland Lake Holiday & Leisure Centre
Signposted from A4 east of Calne.

11. Blakeway Fisheries
Please phone 01934 712532 for details.

12. Bullocks Farm Lakes
4.5 miles from J20 off M5 (Clevedon/Nailsea). Follow signs for B3133 for Yatton. Drive through village of Kenn. Turn right for Kingston Seymore (Fishing lakes signposted). In centre of village turn sharp right into Bade lane and follow signs for Bullock Farm Fishing Lakes.

13. Bush Lakes
Halfway between Notterbridge A 38 & Pillaton or halfway between Hatt & Pillaton.

14. Clawford Vineyard
Take A388 from Holsworthy to Launceston. Turn left at crossroads in Clawton. After 2.5 miles turn left at T junction. Clawford is a further 0.6 miles on left.

15. Cofton Country Holiday Park
From Junction 30, M5 Exeter, take A379 signed Dawlish. Park is on the left half mile after small harbour village of Cockwood.

16. Coombe Fisheries
Leave the A386 (Plymouth to Tavistock road) at Yelverton and then follow signs to Buckland Abbey. The Fishery is signposted 100yds past the Abbey entrance on the left.

17. Coombe Water Fisheries
Half a mile from Kingsbridge on road to Loddiswell, B3210

18. Cranford Inn & Holiday Cottages
Please telephone (01805 624697) for directions

19. Creedy Lakes
Travelling south down the M5 exit at junction 27. From Tiverton take the A3072 Exeter/Crediton road. At Bickleigh bear right towards Crediton. At Crediton town sign, turn right. Follow blue and white fishery signs.

20. Dutson Water and Homeleigh Angling Centre
From Launceston take A388 to Holsworthy. Permits from Homeleigh Angling & Garden Centre, 1 mile from Launceston on A388 on right hand side.

21. Eastcott Lodges
From B3254 take turning signposted North Tamerton. As you come into village take first right to Boyton. Eastcott is 1.5 miles along on the left hand side

22. Elmfield Farm Coarse Fishery
From Launceston take the Egloskerry road found at the top of St.Stephens Hill. About 1 mile out of Egloskerry look for the Treburtle turn off to the right. Follow Fishing signs for 3 mls, signposted on the left.

23. Emerald Pool Fisheries
Off the A38 at West Huntspill, turn into Withy Road by the Crossways Inn. Take the next right Puriton Road. Travel along road for aprox 0.5 mile, over Huntspill river, take the next track on the left. Pool on the right at the top of the track.

24. Fishponds House
From Honiton take the road signposted Dunkeswell & Luppitt. At top of hill bear right signposted Luppitt & Smeatharpe. RAC sign at Luppitt common crossroads "Fishponds House" arrow pointing right. Exactly six miles from Honiton to Luppitt common crossroads

25. Forda Lodges
Follow signs to Tamar Lakes. For further details telephone (01288) 321413

26. Gold Oak Farm
Exit M3. Continue along A31 Ringwood to Verwood follow signs to Heavy Horse Centre. Continue 0.5mile, at T junction turn left, we are signposted 200 yards on left

27. Gwinear Pools
Leave Newquay on A3075 signposted to Redruth. We are on the right hand side 3 miles from Newquay

28. Hazelwood Park
Just off the A379 road from the Exeter bypass, travelling through Starcross, turn left at the Harbour Bridge at Cockwood. The park stands to the right of the Coast road approximately .75mile from the bridge. If using the M5 leave at the exit for Dawlish (junction 30).

29. Hendra Farm
Enter Cornwall on either on A38 (Plymouth) or the A30 (Exeter - Okehampton), which is the better road. At Bodmin A38 joins the A30, follow this to the Perranporth 3285 sign, a mile past the windmills at Carland Cross. Turn on to the Perranporth road and take right hand turn towards Newquay

Directions

in Goonhavern. 300yards out of village turn left by sign to Newperran Campsite. Bear right after 0.75mile at T junction. Hendra is down the left hand lane at the bottom of hill.

30. Houndapitt Farm Cottages
Leave M5 at junction 27. Follow signs to Barnstaple, then Bude until you reach Kilkhampton. Carry on through the village follow signs to Sandymouth, then Stibb. Then turn off to Sandymouth Beach is .5 mile from Stibb, then follow our signs.

31. Kingslake Fishing Holidays
From Okehampton at lights turn right onto A386 to Hatherleigh. At Hatherleigh (7 miles) take left onto A3072 Holsworthy/Bude. Travel 7 miles then turn left at sign 'Chilla 2 miles' Kingslake is .75 mile along this road on left.

32. Little Allers
From Exeter: Take Wrangaton Cross exit off A38, take 2nd road on left. From Plymouth: Take Ivybridge exit off A38. Go through Ivybridge to Wrangaton. Turn right and take 2nd road on left.

33. Little Comfort Farm
2 miles after Braunton turn right at Heddon Mills, at second crossroads,1.8 miles turn left, at next crossroads turn left. Continue 1 mile over bridge then turn right for the fishery.

34. Longleat and Shearwater
From Warminster take 362 towards Frome, follow signs to Longleat. Further information from the bailiff, Nick Robbins on (01985) 844496.

35. Lovelynch Fishery
4 mls from Wellington & 0.5 ml from Milverton. 7 mls from M5

36. Mellonwatts Mill Coarse Fishery
From St. Austell take A390 Truro road to end of Sticker bypass, then road signposted Tregoney and St. Mawes. Turn left after 1 ml for Mevagissey. Fishery 2nd farm on right.

37. Middle Boswin Farm
Take the Scorrier exit off the A30, follow signs to Helston (B3297) through Redruth. Take the B3297 for approx 5 miles passing Four Lanes, Nine Maidens, Burras and Farms Common. Turn left at the sign to Porkellis, follow for less than one mile. Turn left after White Bridge. We are half a mile on the left.

38. Milemead Fisheries
From Tavistock take B3362 (old A384) towards Launceston. Take turning left just outside Tavistock signposted Mill Hill. Entrance is 1 mile down lane on right.

39. Mill Park Touring Site
Take A399 coast road between Ilfracombe and Combe Martin. Take turning opposite Sawmills Inn for Berrynarbor, Lake and touring site are on the left.

40. Millbrook
Approach Millbrook on B3247, follow brown Tourist Signs on right. We are also signposted from Whitsand Bay coastal road.

41. Millhayes Fishery
2 miles from junction 28 (M5) on the A373 towards Honiton turn left at Post Cross to Kentisbeare. 1 mile to village centre, turn left at Post Office and go down hill for 300yds, turn right at sign for Millhayes.

42. Minnows Camping & Caravan Park
From the North or South exit M5 at junction 27 onto A361 signposted Tiverton. After about 600 yards take first exit signposted signposted Sampford Peverell. Turn right at next roundabout, cross bridge over A361. Straight across at next roundabout signposted Holcombe Rogus. Site is on left. From N. Devon on the A361 - go to end of A361 to junction 27 of the M5. Go all the way round and return back onto the A361. Then follow the above directions.

43. New Barn Angling Centre
A385 Totnes to Paington road, follow brown tourist signs, we are opposite Bislades.

44. New Forest Water Park
From Ringwood head towards Fordingbridge on A338. After 4 miles you will see our signs on the left.

45. Oaktree Carp Farm & Fishery
From Barnstaple take the A361 to Newtown. Left onto B3227 Bampton Road for 2.5 miles and left at fishery signpost. Down hill and entrance signposted on right. From M5 junction 27 take A361 to Newtown, then as above.

46. Osmington Mills
Approaching from Wareham on the A352 Dorchester road turn left at the A353 Weymouth junction.. At the Osmington Mills sign opposite the Garage, turn left and follow the lane to Holiday Park. Approaching from Weymouth, follow the A353 Wareham road. Pass through Osmington village and turn right at the sign for Osmington Mills. Follow lane to Holiday Park.

47. Oxenleaze Farm Caravans & Coarse Fishery
From M5, exit at junction 25 & take A358 (s/post Minehead) through Taunton. TakeB3227 (s/post Wiveliscombe, Barnstaple) and turn right at traffic lights in Wiveliscombe. Right again in centre (s/post Huish Champflower) and follow road through Langley Marsh. Shortly after entering Huish Champflower, take the first left turn (signposted Upton), then after approx 1.5mile take next left by white cottage (s/post Chipstable/Raddington). After approx 3/4 mile cross straight over at cross roads and take next right (approx 1/4 mile). Oxenleaze will be found on left in approx 1/2 mile.

48. Pallington Lakes
(Best approached off B3390 at Waddock Cross) Warmwell - Affpuddle Road.

49. Plantation Lakes
From Bristol - Weston-Super-Mare A370. Turn towards Yatton B3133 at Congresbury traffic lights. Go right through Yatton. Turn left towards Kingston Seymour. Just after the Bridge Inn. At village take middle lane. From M5. junction 20. Clevedon. Turn left at both roundabouts onto B3133 towards Yatton, after approx 3 miles turn right towards Kingston Seymour. At village take middle lane.

Directions

50. Retallack Waters
Just off the A39 between Newquay and Wadebridge at Winnards Perch, signposted 'American Theme Park'.

51. Riverton Lakes
M5 junction 27 - Barnstaple via A361. Continue for 3 miles past junction A399 for Lynton then turn right towards West Buckland. 250m left signed Riverton. Barnstaple A361 - Exeter. 1 mile - Landkey & Swimbridge. Signed Riverton. Exeter A377 - Barnstaple. At Kingsnympton B3226 - South Molton - Barnstaple via B3226 & A361. Right - West Buckland. 250m left signed Riverton.

52. Rood Ashton Lake
Leave A350 heading through West Ashton Village. Take next left signposted Rood Ashton, continue to East Town Farm, turn left. Home Farm is 0.5 mile on your left where you will see our sign.

53. Rosewater Lake
Take the A30, follow B3285 through Goonhavern to Perranporth. Continue for .50 mile then turn right for Rose, signposted from crossroads.

54. Royalty Fishery
Royalty & Winkton fisheries main entrance is on B3073, 200yds from it's own junction with A35.

55. Salmon Hutch Fishery
A377 to Crediton, turn left after Shell Garage, follow road signed Tedburn St Mary for 1.5 miles, right at junction marked Uton, follow fishery signs.

56. Sevington Lakes
Situated in the little hamlet of Sevington 1.5 miles from Castle Combe, 2 miles from Yatton Keynell. Accessed from M4 junction 17, follow Kington St. Michael through village & turn left after passing motorway services to Sevington, 1 mile from A420 through Yatton Keynell

57. Sharkey's Pit
Take A30 to Hayle. Two mini roundabouts take first left into Guildford Road. Continue under viaduct. Take 1st right, then 1st left into Strawberry Lane. Continue for approx 0.75 mile. look out for our Fishery sign. We are on the right.

58. Shillamill Lakes
Lanreath, Looe. From Bodmin, take A38, turn right by Dobwalls onto B3359 past East Taphouse. Shillamill signposted on right. Tel: (01503) 220886.

59. Silverlands Lake
Please telephone (01249) 730244 for directions.

60. Simpson Valley Fishery
1.5 miles from Holsworthy on main A3072 Holsworthy to Hatherleigh road.

61. Slapton Ley National Nature Reserve
Enquire at Field Centre in Slapton Village, 0.50 mile off A379.

62. South View Fishery
From Bristol follow M5 onto A38. After 1.5 miles turn off into Kennford. Continue through village following Dunchideock signs until Shillingford signs are seen. Follow Shillingford signs. Entrance to fishery on left at sharp bend before village. From Plymouth turn left off A38 following Dunchideock road until Shillingford signs. From Exeter follow signs to Alphington then Shillingford St. George. Fishery on right after village.

63. South West Water - Coarse
a Slade. b Jennetts. c Darracott. d Melbury. e Trenchford. f Upper Tamar. g Squabmoor. h Old Mill. i Crafthole. j Porth. k Boscathnoe. l College. m Bussow. South West Water fisheries are well signposted from major roads.

64. Spires Lakes
Take the A3072 Holiday Route (HR) from Crediton. Spires Lakes are on the left after the first Winkleigh turn off.

65. St Tinney Farm
We are situated exactly 1 mile off the A39 signposted 'Otterham' 10 miles south of Bude.

66. Stowford Grange Fisheries
Launceston to Lewdown on old A30. Turn at the Royal Exchange pub. 0.5mile along road come to church, bear right. Lake entrance 400 yards.

67. Tanhouse Lake
M4 exit junction 18 onto A46 (Stroud) to Chipping Sodbury on to B4060 Wickwar. Take 4th left to Rangeworthy then Bury Hill Lane. Alternatively M5 to junction to Wickwar to Chipping Sodbury B4060 for 1.5 miles. Take 3rd road on right to Rangeworthy and Bury Hill Lane

68. Thorney Lakes
Directions from A303 to Muchelney. Turn off A303 dual carriageway signposted Martock, Ash. Follow signs to Kingsbury Episcopi, at the T junction in village turn right, through the village of Thorney, over river bridge & disused railway. We are on the left. Thorney Lakes & Caravan Park

69. Town Parks Coarse Fishing Centre
We are half way between Totnes & Paignton along the A385 opposite Charmaine Petrol Station.

70. Tredidon Barton Coarse Fishery
Easily found 4 miles west of Launceston, 0.5mile along A395 from Kennards House. Follow signs to Hidden Valley down country lane

71. Trencreek Farm Holiday Park
4 miles south west of St Austell on A390, fork left onto B3287 Trencreek is one mile on, on the left.

72. Trevella
Proceed on A30 as far as Indian Queens, turn right onto A392, follow signs to Newquay until you come to Quintrell Downs roundabout, take signposted Crantock road which brings you to the Trevenper Bridge roundabout. Turn left onto A3075, the Redruth road, for 200yds and you will see Crantock signposted. If you are in Newquay, take A3075 to Redruth for 1.5 miles until you see Crantock signposted. If

Directions

you are approaching us from the West, you will see Crantock signposted from A3075. Follow this road for 1 mile to T junction signed to Newquay, where you turn right and then into Trevella entrance.

73. Upham Carp Ponds
From J30 on M5, take A3052 signposted Sidmouth. After approx 4 miles, after pasing White Horse Inn on right, sign to fishery will be seen on left. Turn left and after 700yds fishery will be found on left hand side.

74. Upton Lakes
Take junction 28 off the M5 into Cullompton centre then left, second left and over the River Culm. The fishery is signposted from here.

75. Waldens Farm Fishery
Off the A36 Salisbury to Southampton road, near Whaddon. Phone for futher details (01722) 710480.

76. Warren Park Farm
A31, just past Ringwood take B3081, about 1 mile fork right to Alderholt. On entering Alderholt turn left into Ringwood Road, as road bears right farm on the left.

77. Wessex Water - Coarse
a Durleigh reservoir. b Blashford Lakes. c Tucking Mill. Please telephone 0845 600 2 600 for further details.

78. Westpitt Farm Fishery
Go past Blundells School. Take left turn signposted Uplowman. At Redwoods Inn continue for approx 1.5 miles, follow road uphill. Turn right immediately after big Oak tree into farm entrance.

79. Witherington Farm Lakes
2 miles out of Salisbury on A36 fork right as duel carriageway starts, then first right again after about 0.5miles. Follow signs for Downton and Stanlynch. Witherington Farm is about 3 miles on the right.

80. Wood Farm Caravan Park
7 miles west of Bridport on A35, entrance off roundabout with A3052 (access to fishing through caravan park).

81. Wooda Farm Park
From the A39 take road signposted Poughill, Stampford Hill, continue 1 mile, through crossroad. Wooda is 200yds on right.

82. Woodacott Arms
Proceed north off the A3072 at Anvil Corner, turn right at Blagdon Moor Cross or proceed south off the A388 at Holsworthy Beacon, turn left at Blagdon Moor Cross. After approx 1.5 miles turn sharp left at Woodacott Cross, we are located immediately right.

83. Woodland Park
From A36 Bath to Warminster road. Turn at Standerwick, by Bell Inn (opposite Frome Market) Follow lanes to Rudge, turn right at Full Moon. Woodland park is on left hand side.

Chub from the Avon at Bath with Pulteney Bridge in the Background. Picture Matt Carter

**DOLTON
WINKLEIGH
N. DEVON
Tel: 01805 804360**

The West Country's Largest
TROUT FISHERY

Est. 1973 - Open all the year

DAY TICKET WATER
Lower Lake - 14 acres   **High Lake - 8 acres**

FREE FISHING
Darch Lake - average 4.5lb   **Magpie Lake - 1lb-1.25lb**

Environment Agency
Licence required

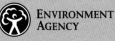 **ENVIRONMENT
AGENCY**

Available at the fishery